OUTSOURCING

TRAINING & EDUCATION

AMERICAN SOCIETY FOR TRAINING & DEVELOPMENT

OUTSOURCING

TRAINING &
EDUCATION

LEARN FROM THE EXPERTS:

COMPREHENSIVE OUTSOURCING

SELECTIVE OUTSOURCING

OUT-TASKING

SUCCESS FACTORS

GARRY J. DEROSE

ASTD

Ordering information: Books published by the American Society for Training & Development can be ordered by calling 800.628.2783 or 703.683.8100.

Library of Congress Catalog Card Number: 99-072435
ISBN: 1-56286-112-3

TABLE OF CONTENTS

PREFACE

The experiences of the companies described in this book, as well as others, yield rich opportunities for learning. For those who seek to undertake an outsourcing project, either as a customer or as a supplier, there is particular value in probing the combined knowledge presented here. The number of outsourcing projects that have been attempted over the past five or six years is relatively small, and the number that have survived is even smaller.

Because so few long-term, successful outsourcing projects exist in the realm of training, education, and development, little of the formal research in this area has been validated. Thus the approach in this book has been to mine the wisdom from CCFL's collective experiences with some of its lengthiest partnerships: Quest Diagnostics, Corning, and Berlex. These are known quantities that have stood the test of time. Similarly, we have plumbed the experiences of several other notable outsourcing efforts through in-depth interviews with partnership managers and providers: Dow Chemical and Delta College Corporate Services; Compaq and Training & Development Systems; and Kaiser Permanente and its five outsourcing partners. These learnings have been tested against the published literature and conference presentations from the training and development professional community and beyond.

In addition to this information, I have drawn from my own personal depth of experience in other functions in order to provide a broad-based rational context. Like any new phenomenon, outsourcing has been subject to hype, and I have attempted to differentiate the underlying rationale and experience from the sweeping generalizations that often make headlines and can mislead even discerning professionals. As a veteran of some 30 years in the training and education field, and one of the first vendors to venture into the outsourcing arena more than a decade ago, I do want to offer encouragement.

I am very grateful to many people who contributed to this book. The substance of two chapters was written by colleagues. Pam Burgess of the Delta College Corporate Services–Dow Chemical partnership provided a chapter that reveals not only the history but also many learnings from the development of that relationship. James Shillaber and Alexandra P. Miller furnished an insightful chapter on the hows and whys of measuring value in outsourcing relationships based on Berlex Laboratories' experience.

In addition, many people contributed to case studies through interviews. My thanks to Debra Turner of Quest Diagnostics; Hans Gutsch, Sandra Fulton, and Karen Monroe of Compaq Computer; Mike Brezina of Training & Development Systems; Madeline Fassler of Kaiser Permanente of Northern California, and Kathryn Arbour, formerly of Kaiser Permanente and now an independent consultant. I am also deeply grateful to the many people with whom I have worked in CCFL's long-standing relationship with Corning Incorporated. Although they are not named in this book, their contributions to my understanding of outsourcing have been deep and significant. Among them are Janet McLaughlin, Ed O'Brien, Sonya Fox, Ed McGarrell, Gail Baity, and many, many more. And to the entire staff at CCFL—thanks immensely for the learning we earn together on a daily basis.

A special word of thanks goes to Laura McGrath whose tireless energy and enthusiasm supported this project in its entirety.

Garry J. DeRose
Corning, NY
April 1999

1

OUTSOURCING: AN INTRODUCTION

1

A WIDELY USED ADDITION TO MANAGEMENT PRACTICES

This book is about outsourcing training and education. The practice of outsourcing this function is so new that it is valuable to view it in a broader context and include some of the lessons learned from other outsourced areas. With this broader context as background, this book will focus on theory and practice in outsourcing the training and education function. It will provide models, processes, and success factors as well as case studies that reflect a range of experiences by those who have charted new paths in this territory.

Outsourcing is a relatively recent word to be added to the corporate vocabulary in North America. And while it is a hot buzzword today, it is very likely that this term will hold a permanent place in the business lexicon. What exactly is outsourcing? For the purposes of this book, it is defined as *transferring to external resources services previously provided internally*. The external supplier assumes major responsibility for a function, including its activities, events, people, and physical assets. This external agency not only oversees the function but also is held accountable for achieving its objectives.

Outsourcing falls into a tradition of customer-vendor relationships, but with some significant differences. There are three key elements that are unique to outsourcing and that distinguish it from traditional customer-supplier relationships. The first is *the nature of the services being supplied by an outside vendor.* In outsourcing, these are very much a part of the fabric of the organization, so much so that managing them internally has generally been assumed to be necessary. The second element that is unique to outsourcing is *the level of responsibility assumed by the supplier.* The supplier becomes accountable for its customer's internal goals—a step well beyond traditional supplier responsibilities. This arrangement, when successful, yields the third unique element: *the extremely close working relationship between customer and supplier.* Management of outsourced services is truly a shared venture.

Today, outsourcing is an important trend in corporate America. Although estimates vary on the size of current efforts, Michael Corbett suggests that outsourcing is seen as an essential management tool used by more than 90 percent of organizations (Bassi et al. 1997). Coopers and Lybrand reports that the trend is prevalent not only among corporate giants but also among small businesses. Of nearly 400 small companies surveyed, with median revenues of $6.5 million and median employment of 66 people, two-thirds used outsourcing. A Gallup survey commissioned by *Training* magazine reveals that 84 percent of the companies surveyed buy some training products or services from outside sources (Gordon 1998). A survey by the Outsourcing Institute estimated that U.S. companies spent $100 billion on outsourcing various business functions (Outsourcing Institute 1998). Corbett suggests that this number will grow to $318 billion by 2001. A 1995 Conference Board survey of 314 large American companies found that 87 percent of them outsource recordkeeping and 59 percent outsource administration and service for their benefits plans (Stewart 1996).

The call to outsource is even greater as top executives look to the future. Surveys have indicated that about half of company decision makers expect to outsource more tasks and functions in the next five years. At one end of the spectrum, a few industry leaders have a vision of organizations in which only the core is internal and the majority of activity is outsourced. At the other end, of course, are companies that select a very few tasks from the corporate list and hand these off to an external supplier. But whether they are now considering outsourcing a lot or a little, many are looking seriously at restructuring their organizations to include external suppliers of services that were previously managed entirely in-house. The dollar volume and number of companies involved in outsourcing may be somewhat higher or lower based on the definition of outsourcing and the companies surveyed.

Given its growing impact, it is no surprise that outsourcing is viewed in a variety of ways—from a dire threat to a magnificent opportunity. Regardless of this range of perceptions, these days outsourcing is on the agenda for some form of consideration in nearly every major corporation.

THE BEGINNING

Outsourcing is, of course, not entirely new. Subcontracting or outsourcing is a consistent thread through the history of business and industry. Computer service bureaus provided support in financial and operational areas as early as the mid-1960s. Their success is evident in the fact that outside providers now cut an estimated 25 percent of all paychecks issued in the United States, and companies like Automatic Data Processing have been growing at double-digit rates for years (Stewart 1996).

In the 1980s, however, outsourcing became something more. As competition increased, American companies reengineered their organizations, reduced head counts, and began to consider their strategic advantages, pricing, and costs in newly rigorous ways. As a part of such strategic self-analyses, they developed an understanding of their corporate core competencies and critical resources. Corporations streamlined and sharpened their strategic focus. As they did so, they began to look with a fresh perspective at anything that was not a core competency or an element critical to their strategic direction. At the same time, new communication technologies made possible "virtual" organizations in which multiple participants could share information at varying locations. In such an environment, corporations began to view outsourcing as a logical alternative to existing work structures.

The current outsourcing route had its major starting point in information systems, but success and publicity brought it to manufacturing, logistics, and eventually to human resources (HR), and finally to training and education. Continental Bank and Kodak were among the earliest to use external suppliers for their information technology. Cummins Engine and Nike were among the early—and highly successful—manufacturing firms that outsourced nonstrategic manufacturing operations. In fact, Nike outsources 100 percent of its shoe production and manufactures internally only key technical components of its Nike Air system. Their extensive, strategic, and skillfully managed outsourcing plan has enabled Nike to create maximum value by concentrating its internal resources on preproduction (research and development) and postproduction activities such as marketing, distribution, and sales (Quinn and Hilmer 1994).

The application of outsourcing to HR has taken place in stages. It was easiest to imagine its use in areas that had clear systems and operational approaches—services such as outplacement, and salary and benefits. And this was precisely where the first HR outsourcing efforts took place. Even before the days of reengineering, when corporations simply mandated sizable, across-the-board layoffs as a means of cost-cutting, firms were established to handle the outplacement of terminated employees. Outplacement services like Career Development Services offered real expertise: a professional mix of personal counseling and employment counseling, often supplemented with a physical support system including offices, telephones, and support staff services for the temporary use of their clients. The success these firms had in placing former employees—and the good will that success bought—took some of the sting out of massive layoffs. In many cases, the impact of using outplacement agencies was so positive that they were retained as permanent adjuncts to the corporate HR staff. Thus, as managers found employees who just were not working out, they were much more comfortable making the sound business decision to let these people go, buoyed by the knowledge that they soon would be employed again. With the advent of reengineering, the use of such services became more widespread.

Even with such successes, however, it was harder to envision accepting and applying outsourcing in areas that HR saw as affecting employee growth or organizational development. These areas seemed sacred, as they contained in the minds of professional HR staff the soul and the conscience of the corporation. The training and education function was clearly one of these. In many organizations, this function was the primary tool for remediation of employee deficits and development of new skills. In addition, many companies saw training and education as the primary vehicle of organizational change, and they developed curricula that were seen as quickening the pulse of the organization. A few innovators, however, saw various opportunities to focus on their business strategies, cut costs, and even improve service by turning over even these sensitive areas to external resources. That number is clearly growing. A 1996 study by the Manufacturers Alliance revealed that, of the firms they surveyed, only 13 percent delivered training entirely in-house. Eighty-three percent outsourced some aspects of their training and education function, and 3 percent outsourced the entire function (Bassi et al. 1997).

THREE CATEGORIES OF OUTSOURCING

Within the broad definition of outsourcing, there are several models. This book will talk about these in three broad categories: comprehensive outsourcing, selective outsourcing, and out-tasking. A review of myriad examples of outsourced training and education, however, has made one thing abundantly clear: This is a dynamic process. Companies that begin by out-tasking a single course or function may use this limited experience as a test and then move to a much broader outsourcing effort. Other firms that boldly develop comprehensive partnerships and outsource the entire function may reengineer this process and reconfigure their supplier arrangements. And within the broad range of companies that selectively outsource, the balance of internal versus external may shift frequently, as needs and opportunities shift. Despite the mobility of these arrangements, it is useful to categorize the process into these models, recognizing not only that companies will slide from one to another but also that there are significant variations and some overlap within and between models.

At one end of the continuum, a few companies have chosen to turn over their entire training and education function to one or more external suppliers. This is called *comprehensive outsourcing*. In this model, an external supplier provides, on an ongoing basis, all aspects of the training function, from the design and development of curricula and training products, to the delivery of training to employees, to the posttraining evaluation. Services like registration, financial accounting for the function, and reporting on a variety of measures also are provided externally. Dupont is one of the best known examples of total outsourcing. They have created a separate entity made up of internal employees and external training resources. This entity is responsible for everything from daily training operations to long-term planning and results. The combination of internal expertise and external objectivity is seen as the key to this successful venture (Bassi et al. 1997).

At the other end of the continuum are companies that use external sources to supply one or more carefully selected, discrete areas. This might be the instruction of a course or a circumscribed curriculum, or it might be a function, such as registration. This very limited and carefully controlled model is *out-tasking*. More and more frequently, firms that have contracted with an external vendor for such a service are now expanding on this concept as a first step toward selective outsourcing. In other firms where particular identified needs seldom change, however, the out-tasking arrangement is relatively stable. For example, one manufacturing firm has an ongoing need for statistics courses. Since the company's plants are relatively small and geographically dispersed, it has long been more effective and cost-effective for them to contract with the vendor to supply these courses than to develop an internal capability. For training in specific manufacturing processes, corporate policies, and many other areas, however, this same company has maintained its own internal training department.

In the middle between these extremes is a range of substantive partnerships in which companies transfer multiple aspects of the training and education function to one or more external suppliers. In these *selective outsourcing* arrangements, the function is largely managed externally, but the working relationship remains very close, and some limited, key areas of responsibility are retained internally. Since this model is the most widely used, it will, in large measure, be the focus for what follows. Variations on this kind of partnership are the subjects of three of the five cases discussed in chapters 4 through 8.

In addition to the terms used to identify these three major models of outsourcing, there is a collection of other terms in current use that further refine, clarify, or confuse the concepts: *preferred provider, sole provider, partner, alliance,* and *shared services.* These will be defined in the context of the models and examples, as it becomes useful to do so.

A GROWING UNDERSTANDING

As with so many business tools, outsourcing was greeted initially as the solution to all major troubles. When the first major articles and examples were published in the early 1990s, the potential benefits seemed limitless. The successes of Cummins Engine, Continental Bank, and Kodak argued for expanded application. Providing a sure sign of a growing business trend, many vendors renamed their services "outsourcing" as they saw a market expansion, and consultants flocked into the field with various systems and tools. Nevertheless, the application of outsourcing to training lagged behind the rest of the market. The exceptions to this were two cases: In the late 1980s, Motorola and Corning had already moved parts of their training function to external organizations, unaware of theory or trend. It simply made sense within their specific training situations.

During the first wave of publicity that surrounded outsourcing, the doctrines, ideas, and processes seemed crystal clear. First, a company or organization needed to define its sources of strategic advantage. That is, it was to define those areas that would most directly affect its ability to achieve its mission—generally, to undertake those actions that would most influence its profitability. Often this was linked to an assessment of its core competencies: those corporate capabilities that were unique, and usually contributed to its strategic direction as well. Once these analyses were completed, the next step was to review its nonstrategic functions or competencies as candidates for outsourcing.

After outsourcing, the enterprise would be able to focus strategically on the core competencies most valued by its customers and most effectively provided by its own internal organization. All other services would be provided by equally focused and effective external providers. Internal and external services would be coordinated to maximize quality, efficiency, and return-on-investment. A careful process could create a virtual organization—a jigsaw puzzle with pieces fitted together to form a tidy work of art. Proponents offered comfort and built confidence by underscoring that outsourcing resembled Japanese approaches where, for example, outsourcing accounts for 30 percent of manufacturing costs and is said to reduce them by 20 percent.

Equally predictable as the first wave of enthusiasm for a new business tool was the reaction against it. A spate of articles appeared that talked of hollowing out the corporation and losing core skills. The specter of overseas dependence caused some alarm: What if North American companies suddenly looked to Japan for training, as the auto and computer industries had sought manufacturing expertise early on? In addition, some hard evidence demonstrated that outsourcing was more difficult than first imagined, and some of the results yielded real disillusionment. A flurry of warnings and complaints appeared about the expense of project changes, the difficulty of constructing and negotiating contracts, and the outsourcing firm being marooned with obsolete technology. Predictably, articles like "The Great Outsourcing Stampede That Never Happened" (Gordon 1998) were published, suggesting that outsourcing was a fad rather than a trend.

In addition, more thoughtful probes of the concepts yielded some tough questions. As businesses analyzed their core competencies, they asked whether internal expertise was sufficient to continue considering their expertise an advantage? They began to ask whether needed expertise would be best developed internally or externally through outsourcing.

The ultimate signal of acceptance of outsourcing was finally indicated when some practitioners, consultants, and researchers began to use a new crop of buzzwords—*selective outsourcing, smart sourcing,* and *insourcing,* to name but a few. These terms embodied the realization that outsourcing works in some situations and does not in others. Ultimately, companies began to acknowledge the following axioms of outsourcing:

- It has to be implemented with care and based on a careful analysis of situation, needs, and desired results.
- It must be managed with skill and evaluated clearly.
- Its benefits can be real but not revolutionary.
- Dangers exist, but disaster is not inevitable.

With experience, there has been a tempering of confidence in the motives and performance of service providers. Companies and suppliers alike have developed a more realistic view of the cost savings that are attainable. The number of those who can attest to outsourcing sharpening strategic focus has increased.

CURRENT VIEW

This wiser, and more balanced, view of outsourcing comes not only from a solid base of experience now being shared but also from independent research. At this point, the major benefits of outsourcing have been identified. They include the following: strategic focus, access to expertise, greater customer responsiveness, faster development, and reduced or stabilized costs. As might be expected, all of these can be attributed to a combination of careful planning, strong, well-defined management, and the quality of the supplier.

Similarly, major drawbacks have been defined. The major ones that surface are concerns over control, the difficulties associated with change, a sense of detachment from an important function, suppliers that are out of touch with the company, excessive costs, and lack of expertise. Again, when problems arise, they are generally linked not just to a single source but to both the customer and the supplier.

Just as there are identifiable benefits and drawbacks for outsourcing in general, some results also are in on the success of various levels of outsourcing. To this point, total outsourcing, in which a company turns over an entire function to one or more external agencies, has had mixed results. On the other hand, considerable success has been documented in both selective outsourcing and out-tasking.

Recent American Society for Training & Development (ASTD) research indicates that out-tasking is now growing rapidly (Bassi et al. 1997).

Outsourcing of major training functions, however, has slowed among leading-edge companies, although it continues to grow among other more cautious adopters. Experience and research have illuminated commonalities among successful outsourcing or out-tasking relationships. No single model fits all or even most situations, but there is a process of investigation that can guide the inquiry. And there are certainly some basic principles that can help to ensure success.

THE PURPOSE OF THIS BOOK

This book offers a close look primarily at successful outsourcing and out-tasking. The second and third chapters outline key elements of how some successful partners have undertaken the outsourcing decision and developed workable processes. Both formal research results and examples are woven into these discussions.

Following these chapters are five extended examples that provide an in-depth look at the practical experiences of companies that are currently outsourcing various aspects of their training and education function. These examples reflect four broad models of outsourcing: comprehensive, administrative, thematic, and multipartner.

In the *comprehensive model,* a company turns over virtually all aspects of training to its partner, although it retains the overall management and direction of the effort. This includes course development and delivery as well as logistics. Typically, the firm retains the planning effort that aligns training with strategic direction, but the partner is often invited to be part of this process.

The *administrative model* is by far the most common arrangement. These contracts may be extensive or very limited, but in effect they turn over some or all of the operational systems to a partner. Registration, billing, supplies, room arrangements, and a multitude of other logistical arrangements are typical services that are outsourced or out-tasked in this model.

The *thematic model* of outsourcing has received considerable attention. In this model, a firm selects a partner based on an alignment between a strong strategic direction of the firm and the vendor's particular competence in that area. This book contains only one example of this model, for good reason— it seldom works. Since training managers so often consider this model when they explore outsourcing, however, it is important to share the experience of one firm that tried it.

Multipartner outsourcing is the newest model. It is most often used by large service organizations that have huge training needs. Often they seek several suppliers who have particular expertise in areas the firms identify: specialized training technologies such as distance learning or videodisc; call-center capabilities for registration and reporting; and well-aligned training content areas such as quality or diversity. Some firms use multiple partners to effect what amounts to comprehensive outsourcing. More typically, however, the firms continue to manage some aspects of their training effort while using several firms to accomplish selective outsourcing.

Specifically, then, here is a quick look at the examples that shed some light on these models. Chapter 4 explores the partnership between Quest Diagnostics and CCFL, a model of comprehensive outsourcing on a somewhat limited scale. The development of this outsourcing partnership has been made easier because it began when Quest began. Chapter 5 provides a look at an arrangement that is probably the most typical outsourcing model in the training world: the selective outsourcing of training logistics. This chapter explains how Dow Chemical partners with Delta College Corporate Services in outsourcing scheduling, materials, course delivery, and other administrative functions. Chapter 6 reveals the permutations that occurred as Compaq initiated and developed its outsourcing arrangements. Like many companies, Compaq started in one direction—in this case, thematic outsourcing—and then made some significant changes in direction before settling into its current partnership with Training & Development Systems. Similarly, Kaiser Permanente's outsourcing experience, discussed in chapter 7, shows the dramatic and extensive changes that occurred in a few short years. What began as a search for a single partner for a comprehensive outsourcing arrangement has metamorphosed to a multipartner model somewhat similar to that used by other huge service industries. The last example reveals how strong and solid an outsourcing relationship can grow over an extended period of time. Chapter 8 focuses on the multifaceted and still-growing relationship between CCFL and Corning—one of the longest-lived outsourcing partnerships in the training world.

At the end of these examples is James Shillaber and Alexandra Miller's seminal chapter on evaluating the outsourcing relationship. In it, the authors explore the model used at Berlex in its partnership with CCFL. Finally, the last chapter summarizes key learnings based on practical experience, and the appendixes contain a variety of tools that may prove useful in the process of decision making, implementation, and evaluation of outsourcing.

All in all, the purpose of this book is to provide a framework, base of experience, benchmarks, processes, tools, and resources, including information on service providers. It is meant to be practical and honest. It is not meant to prescribe a formula by which success can be magically achieved.

And now, without giving away the last chapter, here are three key learnings that will become major themes running throughout the book. The first is that approaching the outsourcing or out-tasking decision and implementation with process steps and tools increases chances of success. The decision to outsource is a business decision; the planning and management of outsourced relationships are business practices. And like all good business decision making, planning, and implementation, the use of a rational process can enable analysis, promote objectivity, and facilitate smooth, quality functioning.

The second key learning is that when the training and education function is outsourced, the company's responsibility for managing learning does not go away; outsourcing is a marriage, not a separation. It is tempting to approach outsourcing with the view that some tasks can be crossed off the corporate list. And indeed they can. But it is also critical to remember that companies are dynamic organizations, with constantly changing needs. This alone would be sufficient reason to maintain a close relationship with the supplier(s). There is, however, another, equally important reason. Training is, in most situations, a critical employee-performance strategy. Thus its development and the measurement of its effectiveness must never be totally displaced from the nerve center of the corporation.

The third key learning is that successful outsourcing depends absolutely on the two partners developing and sustaining a major investment of analysis, effort, and energy, based on mutual trust and utterly dependent on strong communication. This speaks to the need to make a careful choice at the beginning of the relationship and then to nurture and develop it deliberately. It means agreeing to maintain processes for analysis, feedback, and constant, open communication. It means knowing one another very well. With this ongoing investment, the partners can solve problems, anticipate needs, and design and implement improvements. Without it . . . well, there is entirely too much left to chance. And like rocky marriages, sometimes the partners simply wake up one morning and discover a stranger lying next to them.

So there are pitfalls. But there are also some guides to success, which will largely form the content of this book. In all, when it works, outsourcing requires an element that goes beyond a good contract and clearly defined services. It requires the blurring of organizational lines, the growth of trust, the development of a long-term relationship, and a strong mutual commitment to one another's success. At once elegantly simple and bewilderingly complex, outsourcing is the challenge—and the prize—for those who make continuous improvement a way of doing business.

References

Bassi, Laurie, Laurie Buchanan, and Scott Cheney. (1997). "Outsourcing Training." In *Trends That Affect Learning and Performance Improvement: A Report to the Members of the ASTD Benchmarking Forum.* (3d edition). Alexandria, VA: American Society for Training & Development.

Gordon, Jack. (1998, February). "The Great Outsourcing Stampede That Never Happened." *Training,* 38–48.

Quinn, James Brian, and Frederic G. Hilmer. (1994, Summer). "Strategic Outsourcing." *Sloan Management Review,* 43–55.

Stewart, Thomas A. (1996, 15 January). "Taking on the Last Bureaucracy: People Need People—but Do They Need Personnel?" *Fortune,* 105.

The Outsourcing Institute. The outsourcing index. Cited 17 November 1998. http://www.outsourcing.com/news/dnb/.

2

THE PROCESS OF
OUTSOURCING

2

OVERVIEW

As consulting groups have begun to provide outsourcing services, their prospective customers have utilized a variety of systems for deciding whether or not to outsource, and if so, how to go about it. This chapter will present the six-step process that CCFL (College Center of the Finger Lakes) has developed and used successfully. Other models have anywhere from three to six steps. The version proposed by edcor Data Services has six steps: strategic analysis, identifying the best candidates, defining requirements, selecting providers, transitioning the operations, managing the relationship. DDI (Development Dimensions International), on the other hand, boils it down to three: decide, select, and contract. Although these clearly vary on the specifics included, the best conceptual models have three elements in common. The first is a methodology for analyzing functions (and areas within functions) in order to determine which are critical and which are not. The second is a process that enables users to decide the best way to source those functions, matching activities with sourcing options. The third is an approach both to establishing an alliance and to managing the resulting outsourcing relationship over time to ensure results.

While called "steps," these process stages are not a recipe. Following them to the letter will not lead an organization to some uniform result. Instead, the process provides a framework that is best used when it is thoughtfully manipulated to fit each organization's needs, culture, purpose, and other particular circumstances. In addition, while some steps or actions described within them are sequential, others can be done simultaneously, and still others need to recur at several points.

Here are a couple of examples of such situations. A crisis in the platform that supports a firm's registration system might create such urgency that the first step would be to identify prospective vendors. Conceivably, the company might need to learn about various capabilities and technological fits within the vendor's information technology (IT) system before it was possible to select the specific activities to outsource. This need would mean that Step 2: Select Activities, and Step 3: Choose Vendor(s), would need to fall in reverse order. In another example, a company's team might need to consider some issues, like trust building and a people strategy, long before Step 5: Transition, where the discussion of them falls in this chapter. Such scenarios only begin to suggest the complexities of each business situation and the resulting need for a process that can be meaningfully adapted to fit them.

This chapter begins with a thumbnail sketch of the six steps. Then each step will be developed in more detail. Included in these discussions are examples and learnings, as well as brief descriptions of some common process tools that aid in carrying out the steps and actions.

THE OUTSOURCING DECISION PROCESS

The six steps that make up the outsourcing decision process are as follows: commit, select activities, choose vendor(s), contract, transition, and manage and improve.

1. **Commit.** At the beginning, the decision makers responsible for sourcing an area need to make a commitment to selecting and implementing the best sourcing decision. At this early stage, core members of a team are identified. They develop a macro view, articulating broad goals, taking an honest look at options, and candidly discussing hopes and fears for what these changes might mean. Based on this information, the team members develop a sourcing strategy. They outline a project plan, including a timeline, and articulate the business case for their decision. This is the groundwork that makes it possible for everyone to start with a common understanding of the situation. Uncovering hidden agendas, addressing fears associated with major change, and clarifying both the process ahead and its expected outcomes are critical aspects of this step. Without such a process step, projects too often begin with hidden agendas, hopes for failure, and a commit-

ment to "directed" restructuring, and they wind up mired in difficulties or, ultimately, failed.

2. **Select Activities.** This step details what has been outlined in the commitment step. Selecting activities includes identifying functions or tasks, analyzing sourcing options, and making a preliminary choice about which ones (if any) are the most likely candidates for outsourcing. In this step, the team identifies the full range of sourcing options—internal, contractual, and consulting—for each activity. The list of potential activities to be considered for outsourcing varies by situation.

3. **Choose Vendor(s).** Here, the effort becomes very specific. The team develops a pool of potential suppliers and the criteria against which to measure each one. By undertaking rigorous analysis based on the organization's needs and the vendors' expertise, an organization (and its prospective vendors) can make a sound decision about *whether, on what,* and *how* best to work together. Thus, not only does this step result in the selection of vendors, it also yields the information critical to begin shaping a contract.

4. **Contract.** The ultimate goal of this step is to negotiate a document that neither party will ever need to consult because, through the contracting process, they have mutually agreed to needs, means, and contingencies. The contract provides guidelines for working together and handles copyrights, office space, and multiple other specific issues. Contracting is fraught with fears, cautions, and warnings, however, so there are some specific concerns to be aware of beforehand. Among other things, the contract should spell out requirements and guidelines to be followed if things do not work out.

5. **Transition.** Once decisions about vendors have been made and key expectations outlined in the contract, the next step is to complete a plan for incrementally moving activities to the supplier(s). The transition plan should include milestones against which to measure progress at regular intervals. At the same time, both the company and the vendor(s) should be on the lookout for surprises and unplanned-for opportunities.

6. **Manage and Improve.** Managing for the long term, the final step, is truly critical, but often overlooked. It is tempting, and often fatal, to assume that once the outsourcing is arranged, a company can walk away and expect the "machine" to operate on its own. Outsourcing is a partnership, and it requires a formal structure, including a partnership manager. Depending on the size and scope of the arrangement, the manager can be a single person or a staff, with full- or part-time responsibilities for various elements of the outsourcing. The point is this: There must be someone in charge, overseeing the operation. An important tool for the project managers on both sides is a system of monitoring and measurement. Measures should be established to correspond with each of the project's goals. A system for feedback is essential to understanding whether the results are meeting those goals. Analysis of this information is a requisite for planning improvement. Evaluation is such a crucial element that a full chapter has been devoted to it, in addition to the action items discussed later in this one.

This, then, is a brief overview of the six-step process recommended for making the decision to outsource and for setting up the systems that will affect its long-term success. The rest of this chapter is devoted to a more in-depth discussion of each of these steps. Each section includes the following: an overview of the topic, a list of some specific actions, and a discussion of each action.

Step 1. Commit

What is involved in committing to the sourcing decision process? Most of the time, the message arrives special delivery: "Outsource!" Sometimes it comes packaged as part of a strategic plan; sometimes it involves a reorientation of the organization; sometimes it is strictly a cost-cutting measure. Whatever the impetus—take on new responsibilities, cut staff, reduce costs—some mandate drives most outsourcing decisions. Except in cases where management offers no options, the very first step should be a commitment to an *open review of sourcing options.* This does not mean an automatic commitment to outsourcing.

Why devote time and energy to a commitment step? Because it is critical to unite the team at the outset, to understand the rationale, to clarify expectations, and to address fears and hidden agendas. One of the team leader's first clear messages should be that everyone must live with the results of fair analysis. Without taking the steps involved in commitment, the team may fail to achieve consensus, and underground conflict likely will erupt and disrupt the process later on. Taking on potential problems at an early stage can cement the team and open the door to creative solutions. Having gotten off to the right start, the team can then develop a planning process and establish broad goals.

Following are the specific actions in the commitment step, which when taken together lay crucial groundwork for the success of the project:

- Describe the business case.
- Build the team; identify hopes and fears.
- Develop a project plan; establish decision diamonds.
- Set overall project goals.

Describe the Business Case

The process begins with a candid discussion of what is behind the impetus to change the present organizational structure or system of delivery. Why is alternative sourcing being considered? What is the current situation in the company, and what strategic directions are influencing decisions for the future? What changes need to happen and why? Typically, this discussion will center on new services, lower costs, adjustments in head count, or increasing competitive advantage. This discussion should remain at a macro level and provide participants with the management's view from 10,000 feet.

One important reason for getting the business case on the table at the outset is that it helps to overcome resistance. Experience shows that higher-level managers warm up to the idea of outsourcing more quickly than those directly involved, partly because they see the big picture. Sharing that larger managerial perspective with the people directly affected does not necessarily prevent them from being unhappy about the decision, but at least it gives them a basis for understanding.

From the beginning, it is helpful to establish that the end goal of the process is not to decide whether or not to outsource, but rather to choose the *best way of sourcing.* The range of options is as wide as with other functions. Vendors can supply services on a temporary basis (as contractors or temporary employees) for flexibility of delivery and timing, or they can supply them consistently over a longer period (either as preferred contractors or preferred vendors), or the service can continue to be supplied internally. A few companies have established their goals and found that by restructuring internally, outside help was not needed. This is the exception, but it does happen. Thus the business case presented to the team needs to include two elements: the rationale behind management's directive and the purpose for alternative sourcing options.

As will be discussed more fully in chapter 8, at Corning the business case focused primarily on the overall corporate strategy. Training and development were to guide organizational change by increasing employees' skills. To do so, the company needed to add to its inventory of leading-edge skills courses. There was also a need to stabilize the head count and costs in the education and training department, however. To address the concerns and confusion that always accompany change, the director of education and training helped both his staff and internal customers prepare to focus on the process ahead. Among his actions were to develop and present a slide show articulating the rationale for outsourcing.

Selling the business case and communicating goals become very important in addressing the concerns and sometimes-hidden agendas of various stakeholders. Understandably, job preservation or control of the function are very important personal and professional issues that can obstruct progress toward re-sourcing. Thus it is very important to address these and build a spirit of open inquiry. Only then is it reasonable to expect a fair analysis. "Seldom was there an unbiased audit to bring accountability to the sourcing process," says Ravi Venkatesan, assistant to the group vice president of operations at Cummins Engine, in his article "Strategic Sourcing" (1992). While he speaks from a manufacturing perspective, the same experiences are true in training and development.

Build the Team

One element of success in the sourcing decision process is choosing the right team and players. The choice of team members should be among the very first commitments—one that sends a message to all involved. Many managers recommend involving top management, as well as the relevant human resources people. In this way, the team can be widened as needed at critical points, and it has the authority to move forward smoothly.

From the outset, the team leader needs to set a tone of complete openness and honesty. It is realistic and often helpful to establish that outsourcing is not a certainty, but that change is. This helps to reinforce the openness of the process as well as to confront the inevitable fears and concerns. It is also wise for the leader to begin by letting people know which decisions have already been made and which are within the team's scope of responsibility. Allowing people to believe that a decision has already been made, when in fact it has not, can result in unintended and undesirable effects, such as lower morale, resentment, or rivalry among departments. On the other hand, if there is no choice, the team also needs to understand that, in order to avoid spinning wheels on issues beyond their control.

Learning: Job Anxiety

In a context of job anxiety and market flux, experience shows that some team members will harbor hopes that certain functions (usually someone else's) will be sent out, while others may desire that the whole search fail. Problems like these can sabotage an outplacement decision-making process before it ever begins.

In any situation involving significant change, fear, anxiety, and various forms of resistance surface. In the case of sourcing analysis, fears typically fall into three categories: personal, departmental, and companywide. The personal concerns focus on jobs. What is going to happen to my job? Will I even have one, or will it change so much that I do not want it or cannot handle it? Beyond this very real and personal concern, people worry for their department. Will we be able to retain our core competencies? Will we be able to deliver relevant and quality service? The fears about the company usually deal with control issues. Will we lose strategic direction in training and education? Will bringing in outsiders create fundamental friction over differences in culture? Will they be able to focus on our customers as well as we do?

Exercise: Acknowledging Fears

With the team, actually go through an exercise with a facilitator and a flipchart to name and record people's goals and anxieties—for themselves and for the organization—then keep it for posterity. It is a clear reference point. Of course, it will not erase personal agendas, but it might flush them out of hiding.

Undertaking a formal exercise to acknowledge fears helps to build acceptance among team members. It enables them to recognize who has (and who does *not* have) authority for various parts of the sourcing decision. The exercise makes it possible to move the process forward by helping all team members start with a common understanding of the situation.

Thus decision makers need to take on the fears as directly as they take on the hoped-for results. The point is not necessarily to eliminate these fears, nor is it to squash hopes. Rather, the purpose is to air them all, allowing people to know that they have been heard and to feel that they are part of an open, honest process. As the players jell into a true team, they are ready to take on the more concrete aspects of the planning process.

Develop a Project Plan

This action makes the commitment tangible. The team acts on its commitment by preparing a framework for the whole process from decision making through implementation. This should include a timeline, the major steps in the process, and the decision diamond points. Among the crucial items to include in the plan is the communication effort.

At this early stage, the plan needs to be very basic. It should outline broad task areas, assign responsibilities, identify milestones and decision diamonds, and establish time frames. Essentially, it will include the six process steps outlined in this chapter, or some variation on them: commit, select activities, choose vendor(s), contract, transition, and manage and improve.

Experience has taught that it is absolutely essential to establish a time frame for each step in the decision-making process. Clearly, sufficient time must be allotted in order to do the work necessary for reaching a sound decision. But it can be harmful to drag it out too long. A protracted process perpetuates anxiety and postpones effective transitions. In most cases, three to six months has proved about the right amount of time to complete the process of making a decision and completing the planning.

The form shown in table 2.1 is a simple planning tool, identifying stages, milestones or decision diamonds, responsibilities, and time frames.

One strongly recommended step in the planning process is establishing the decision diamonds early on. This helps the team to focus clearly on gathering the information and doing the homework needed to reach the key decisions. Certainly the end of every process step should include a decision diamond; it will be important to plan for others at critical stages of the subtasks as well.

Table 2.1. Project Planning Form				
Task	Milestone(s)/ Decision Diamonds	Person Responsible	Communication Plan	Completion Date
Commit				
Select activities				
Choose vendor(s)				
Contract				
Transition				
Manage/Improve				

The decision diamond process (see figure 2.1) entails checking with the project's sponsor, scanning the environment for changes, summarizing learnings and recommendations, and then clarifying the next steps and total process. This results in a formal go-no-go decision before moving on. It is a point of forced reflection, so the process does not take on a life of its own. Instead, the team evaluates the process to date from the necessary points of view, then decides what needs to be modified in the next round. This process also ensures that the team gains buy-in from decision makers, team members, and customers at each critical step. It has the effect of finalizing decisions and

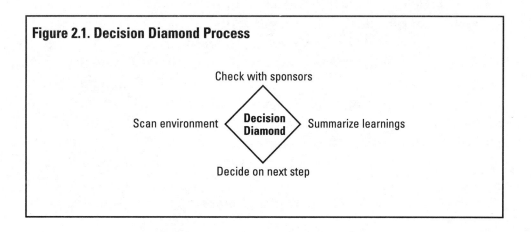

Figure 2.1. Decision Diamond Process

Check with sponsors

Scan environment — Decision Diamond — Summarize learnings

Decide on next step

laying the groundwork for the next building phases so that old issues do not keep resurfacing and undermining the process.

For example, in Step 2 the team will gather a great deal of information about current processes, current suppliers, and potential new vendors. They will also assess the advantages and drawbacks of each. Having completed these tasks, they should be poised to select which activities can be outsourced. The decision diamond forces the team to ensure that all the necessary data is in, that nothing has changed in the environment since they started the process, that key decision makers have signed off, that any overlooked issues are brought in, and that they have synthesized what they learned. With all of these critical points included, they are equipped to decide whether to move forward, and if so, to plan for the next stage: deciding on the vendors and the criteria against which to measure them.

Set Overall Project Goals

As team members develop the big picture for sourcing, they must establish and articulate goals. Often these will be stated or implied in the directive handed down: "Reduce costs," "Streamline staffing," or "Improve quality." As with the project plan, at this point in the process, these goals will likely be very general. Naming the goals clearly is like forming the keel of the boat: They hold the building process together and give shape to what follows.

If, for example, one goal is to acquire cutting-edge technical training, that goal will guide the later development of the specific criteria for measuring vendors. It will also be a key component of the contract. Later on, the team will build on this goal to develop specific provisions for updating the identified skills and the means by which the supplier will handle advances in technology (and all of its associated complexities, including how to deal with costs). In addition, clearly stated goals will become a focal point for managing the partnership and assessing results. All of these later steps rest on the thoughtful, clear development of these early, broad goals.

Setting goals is an iterative process. Once established, the early goals need to be reviewed regularly. In most cases, they will undergo several minor revisions as the process moves forward. Occasionally, however, new information or changes in the environment will require that a goal be changed significantly. Thus, regular review is important.

Keeping the goals in front of the team may seem obvious, but it is overlooked with surprising frequency. The reality of major planning efforts is that the associated turmoil and emotion sometimes obscure the purpose itself.

Holding the goals and the business case in clear view helps the team to chart a steady course forward. With the project plan in hand, the goals and business case outlined, and some hopes and fears out in the open, the team is ready to analyze an education and training department's activities in order to determine the best sourcing solutions.

Step 2: Select Activities

How does the team select what to outsource and what to keep? This step is the heavy-duty analytical stage of the process. Following are the outcomes of the team's analyses:

- an understanding of how—and how well—the department's activities are structured to serve the present and future needs of the company
- a list of areas that could benefit from outsourcing or other new sourcing options
- identification of key improvement opportunities
- baseline measures that will form the groundwork for selecting vendor(s)—the next process step

In this step, the team not only lists all of the organization's functions and activities but also identifies those central activities that make the biggest difference to customers. Next, it identifies various possible sources for those activities, both internal and external. It evaluates the ability of each to deliver in relation to the established goals. Then it makes a tentative decision about which functions and activities to outsource, which to source in other ways, and which to analyze further. Next the team identifies areas for improvement—both for activities that will remain internal and for those that will be sourced externally. Finally, it develops baseline measures (or reexamines current measures, if they exist) for each key activity so that future change can be measured.

This part of the process can be fairly straightforward or exceedingly complicated. The scope of the task depends on two things: (1) the size of both the company and the education and training department; and (2) how closely education and training are linked to achieving key corporate goals or major operational needs like regulatory requirements. In very large, complex organizations like Kaiser Permanente, with multiple sites of operation and training, myriad regulatory requirements, and major new corporate directions, the task of analysis was necessarily huge. Regardless of size and complexity, however, establishing and following a clear plan for analysis are necessary for making sound sourcing decisions.

Team members must perform the following actions in order to produce a clear analysis of the outsourcing process:

- Understand the organization's role in relation to the company's strategic needs and direction.
- List functions and activities, and identify core competencies (those where the organization has unique capabilities or strengths).
- Identify potential sources.
- Review the pros and cons of sourcing alternatives.
- Select activities or functions to outsource (and recommend those to be done by any other alternative means).
- Identify improvement opportunities.
- Set baseline measures.

Understand the Organization's Role

Understandably, people in learning and development organizations often believe that no one else can do what their organization does, or do it as well. Thus it is particularly important to use a decision process that allows the team members to step back and base their decisions on information. This step helps the team focus on which of the department's activities contribute to the company's strategic goals. Those activities that do not advance the company's agenda may be candidates for outsourcing.

A growing body of literature on a wide range of business topics, including outsourcing, includes discussions of strategic decisions and core competencies. Terms like *strategic direction, critical, fundamental, key,* and *core competencies* are used with varying shades of meaning. To avoid getting bogged down in the confusion sometimes associated with this jargon, it is wise to focus on two key ideas.

1. The team members need to understand what their company needs now and in the future. It is particularly important to understand both where the company is headed (direction and goals) and how

it plans to get there (strategies). A copy of the CEO's short- and long-term plan is a good place to begin.

2. Team members also need to understand how the training, education, and development function fits into that picture. Depending on the complexity of the organization, this task may be relatively straightforward, or it may require extensive analysis and soul-searching. Ultimately, the team must distinguish, from a management perspective, which of the services its organization renders are critical to the company's key strategies, and which are less important.

How does the team determine what is strategic? Figure 2.2 reflects a simplified hypothetical example of a manufacturing company. The company's leadership has articulated three key strategies: growing profits, developing new products, and delivering quality. The education and training department has an excellent portfolio of learning opportunities. But a comparison of the learning products with the company's key strategies reveals that four of these areas tie directly to the corporate strategies. Innovation enables new product development. Marketing tools help both to build sales (and therefore profitability) and to launch new products successfully, linking them also to the new

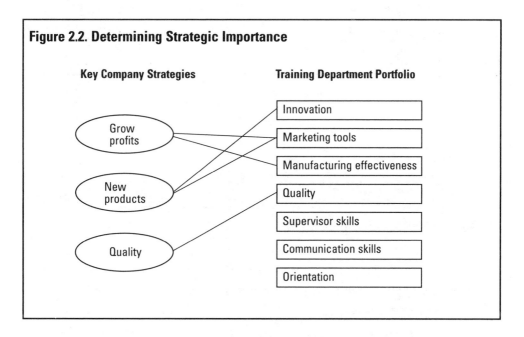

Figure 2.2. Determining Strategic Importance

Key Company Strategies | Training Department Portfolio

Grow profits
New products
Quality

Innovation
Marketing tools
Manufacturing effectiveness
Quality
Supervisor skills
Communication skills
Orientation

product strategy. Manufacturing effectiveness focuses on efficiency, which translates to cost savings and therefore to the corporate strategy of growing profits. The other three areas in the portfolio, although essential to company operations, are not linked to the key corporate strategies.

There are numerous ways to go about such an analysis. The two examples offered here, one from manufacturing (Cummins Engine) and one from information technology (Continental Bank), could easily be adapted to training and education situations.

Example: Manufacturing

In his article "Strategic Sourcing" (1992), Ravi Venkatesan describes the process Cummins Engine used to audit and review various functions, activities, and categories in its manufacturing operation. When he researched manufacturers who outsourced, he was disturbed to find that their decisions had been made without analyzing either the strategic importance of parts or the competence of either the company itself or the various suppliers at manufacturing those parts. Thus he began by analyzing the strategic value of various parts. Cummins defined "strategic" to mean:

- *high impact on customers*
- *requiring specialized design and production skills and physical assets*
- *involving fluid technology*

To avoid the temptation simply to hand off the most difficult processes, Venkatesan expanded the decision matrix to include what was "indispensable to the company's competitive position." This linked Cummins's production processes with its strategic direction.

Example: Information Technology

Continental Bank explored options for outsourcing its information technology function. Continental began by defining activities according to how critical each was in relation to profit. Thus they analyzed their operations according to three broad criteria:

- *profitable and critical to customers*
- *profitable but noncritical to customers*
- *other—ready to be considered for outsourcing*

The two companies' determinations of what is strategically important differ substantially; each reflects the nature of its enterprise and the function subject to re-sourcing considerations. The lists of criteria are likely to differ just as greatly among companies in which training and education activities are the subject of re-sourcing discussions. The important point here is that this process results in a clear understanding of its company's key strategies and provides the basis for the team to determine how its organization contributes to them. Thus such an analytical process yields the first piece of information the team needs in order to select activities that could be outsourced.

Such an analysis can bestow other important benefits as well. In revealing where the training and education organization is aligned with the company's strategies, the analysis also may expose some gaps. For example, in a company focused on innovation, analysis might uncover a void in the company's understanding of how to search out and purchase new product ideas from inventors in universities or incubators. Developing a learning process and appropriate resources to identify and acquire such products might have enormous impact on a key company strategy.

Whether or not this analysis yields such additional benefits, it does give the team one of the bases for deciding which areas should be managed internally, and which might be considered for outsourcing. As the next activity reveals, however, alignment with company strategy is not the only criterion for making the outsourcing decision.

List Functions and Activities

Having compared the department's output with the company's key strategic directions, the next task for the team is to identify their organization's particular strengths and unique capabilities. For the purposes of this discussion, these capabilities will be called core competencies (again recognizing that this term may have different meanings in other contexts). These core competencies can be the activities an organization does particularly well or those that, for various reasons, no other organization could easily duplicate.

There are at least two ways to begin this process. One is to look at the department's functions: course development, instruction, registration, marketing, and so forth. The other is to look at its output: the portfolio of courses or learning opportunities. The team may choose one or the other, or it may decide to look at both. In either case, assessing core competencies means determining what the organization does particularly well—an error-free system for training delivery, or a world-class supervisor effectiveness program, for example. It also involves identifying department activities so unique that replacing them externally would be virtually impossible. These are likely to be systems such as registration or chargebacks that are tied into the company's IT system. But they might also include instructional programs with highly specialized content, such as training in certain unique manufacturing processes.

Learning: Core Competencies

Consulting experience has found it almost universally true that company training and development personnel identify certain of their programs as unique or core competencies when in fact these are extremely similar to packaged programs offered by training organizations. The ones that typically appear in this category are communications, presentation skills, and supervisor effectiveness.

The discovery of such similarities almost always results in disbelief and resistance—not surprisingly, since the employees have typically invested a great deal of energy in ensuring the excellence of these programs. When they benchmark their courses against those available through external resources, however, they almost invariably discover that their programs are not, in fact, unique, and that while they may be delivering a world-class product, so are several prospective suppliers.

The key learning from these experiences is that when such areas are identified, the process of benchmarking is extremely helpful in gaining some perspective. Such a process can enable the team to assess objectively those particular areas that they may see as core competencies, but that are not strategically important.

Table 2.2 shows how a hypothetical team assessed which of its functions and which of its portfolio of services were core competencies. The latter is the same portfolio of services that previously was compared to key company strategies in figure 2.2.

Table 2.2. Core Competency Analysis

Department Functions	Core comp	Department Output (Portfolio of Services)	Core comp
Registration/billing	Yes	Innovation	Yes
Course delivery/logistics	Yes	Marketing tools	No
Instructional design/development	No	Manufacturing effectiveness	Yes
Instructor selection and management	No	Quality	Yes
Managing external training suppliers	Yes	Supervisor skills	No
Marketing	No	Communications skills	Yes
Facilities management	Yes	Orientation	Yes

Having completed the two analyses shown in figure 2.2 and table 2.2—strategic fit and core competencies—the team now has the essential information it needs to make preliminary outsourcing decisions and now can complete the decision analysis by putting each activity into one of three broad categories:

- keep internal
- ready to outsource
- further study

As the diagram in figure 2.3 depicts, activities that both contribute to the firm's key strategies and are core competencies for the department are good prospects to be kept internally. Clear candidates for outsourcing will be those activities that are aligned with neither strategies nor core competencies. The activities that may need further study are those that are either aligned with strategies, but are not core competencies, or those that are core competencies but are not aligned with strategies.

This model is based on an approach that matches internal resources with company strategies. At the same time, it capitalizes on the department's strengths and unique capabilities. While the model may be more useful in dealing with the department's portfolio of services and courses than with its functions, these begin to fall into place.

Of course, there may be situations in which the best decision contradicts the model. In most cases, however, this process yields objective information on which to base sound decisions. One of its benefits is that it allows the

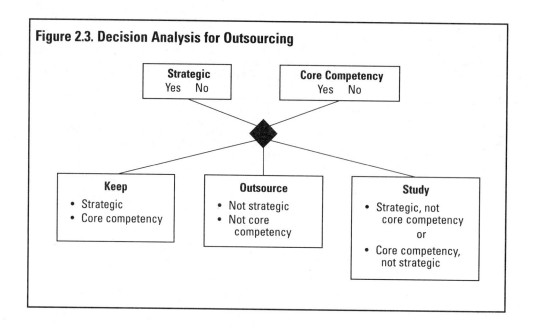

Figure 2.3. Decision Analysis for Outsourcing

Strategic	Core Competency
Yes No	Yes No

Keep
- Strategic
- Core competency

Outsource
- Not strategic
- Not core competency

Study
- Strategic, not core competency

or

- Core competency, not strategic

entire team—and ultimately the management and customers—to view the sourcing recommendations from a rational perspective. In so doing, it helps to prevent emotions or turf issues from disrupting the process or driving the decisions.

Learning: Outsourcing Strategic Functions

An example from manufacturing provides the exception that proves the rule. Cummins Engine decided to outsource the manufacture of pistons—a key strategic part. In benchmarking four of the world's best piston manufacturers, they discovered that their own capabilities fell below all of these others. The lesson here is that even though an area may be of enormous strategic importance, someone else may do it better than the internal department.

Although the decisions to keep or outsource should not be considered inviolable, at this point, most of a team's time will likely be devoted to the third category in figure 2.3—"study." It might be tempting for a company to keep all of its core competencies—whether or not they are strategic—and outsource the rest. Experience has shown, however, that selective outsourcing or out-tasking typically yields better results than complete outsourcing.

It is very likely that some core competencies will be moved quickly to the "keep" category, even though they are not strategic. Certain functions are likely to appear on that list, and there may be some services that will appear there as well. For example, training for unique manufacturing processes that undergo frequent improvements or upgrades might be very difficult to hand off, even though they may have no bearing on key strategies, and may not even be core competencies. Other items might move to the "outsource" category, even though they are aligned to strategies. An example of such a situation might be quality training. Although this program may align directly with a key strategy, there are now a number of training firms with excellent quality programs. Such firms regularly tailor their approach to their customers' specific needs and cultures. If one of the goals is to reduce head count, such a large program might be migrated to the outside, despite its alignment to strategy and perhaps even the education and training department's history of success with this program.

For other items in the "study" category, however, the answers may not come so easily. Among the questions that can help teams to sort through the tough issues in this category are: How much investment would it take to make a strategically important service into a core competency of the education and training department? Can an outside vendor provide a similar service with no loss of quality or control? Even while team members delve into the "study" list, they can begin to use the body of objective information and preliminary decisions to continue their analysis. One of the important aspects of this is to analyze the probable impact of the proposed changes.

Learning: Outsourcing Whole Functions

In an extreme example, outsourcing whole functions within IT has left some companies without the critical skills and knowledge necessary to evaluate trends and proposed changes in their own presumed core competencies. This is the most profound fear of most managers: hollowing out their organizations to the extent that they lose the ability to accomplish their job. Thus it is extremely important to manage the ongoing direction of the function internally.

In their article "The Value of Selective IT Sourcing" (1996), Mary Lacity and her coauthors provide additional questions that can help teams assess the impact of proposed outsourcing, such as the following:

- Are the requirements in this category expected to change? If so, it will be important to develop a plan for how to address the changing situation. If a potential partner will have to deal with substantive change, that should be built into the contract. Better still, such a migration might better wait until the situation has stabilized.

- Can this function be broken off cleanly? Split processes have a high rate of failure or error.

- Does the department understand the function clearly enough to be able to manage its delivery by an outside provider? Outsourcing does not mean walking away from a function or task; it means continuing to oversee it in a new form.

- Can the team write a contract that will include requirements, minimize risks, and provide flexibility?

- Does the department's current staff have sufficient knowledge and skill to effectively negotiate, get the most from the contract, and deal with vendor change?

With the information and preliminary decisions yielded by these analyses, the team can move on to the rest of the actions recommended for Step 2: search out potential sources, review the pros and cons of sourcing alternatives, identify improvement opportunities, and set baseline measures.

Identify Potential Sources

Finding external resources may be among the easiest tasks on the team's list. In many cases, the training department may already have relationships with one or more suppliers. In addition, many training managers participate in the American Society for Training & Development (ASTD) and other professional associations for people who work in the training and development field. These organizations' publications and conferences provide opportunities to learn about some of the larger and better-known training firms. In addition, colleagues met by networking through such organizations are usually very willing to share information about their firms' experiences with various resources, and may also provide opportunities for benchmarking various outsourcing arrangements.

For some firms and situations, geography may be an important factor. In large metropolitan areas, the team may choose to use regional training councils, chambers of commerce, or other business associations to identify resources. In smaller communities, it may be simpler to contact directly the short list of options. Again, colleagues in other companies can often provide invaluable insight and information based on their experiences with these resources.

Review Sourcing Alternatives

Within the broad categories of internal or external sourcing are multiple considerations that may influence the final decision. Among the internal options are: keeping the current structure and staff, reorganizing the structure and staff, hiring new personnel, and merging certain functions or tasks with similar groups in other departments. The external options include outsourcing, out-tasking, or contracting discrete tasks or courses.

There are advantages and disadvantages to each scenario, and it is important to weigh each of them as accurately and objectively as possible. Table 2.3 provides some general observations for each of the categories. These observations can provide some guidance for the more specific task of analyzing each sourcing decision. Beyond that, the team can use the structure provided

Table 2.3. Pros and Cons of Sourcing Alternatives				
	Advantages	**Disadvantages**	**Corporate Role**	**Cost**
Outsource	• Expertise • Comprehensive services • Focus • No head count • Flexible • Self-managing	• Heavy time investment in start-up • Complex	• Manage partnership • Manage learning function	High initial cost; lower operational costs
Internal	• Control • Supervision • Permanent • Build competencies	• Increase head count	• Manage staff • Provide training	High start-up; long-term financial obligation
Contract	• Project management • Specific skills	• Fragmented operation • Lack of employee commitment	• Manage staff • Supervise projects	Premium for flexibility; no commitment

Source: DeRose/Brezina

in this table in analyzing each of the re-sourcing options—or at least the more difficult ones. Here it will be important to weigh not only the advantages and disadvantages of each decision, but to do so in context of the goals established at the beginning of the sourcing decision process.

For example, if reducing permanent staff is a major goal, that may outweigh other factors in deciding the number and scope of services to be sourced externally, either through outsourcing or through limited contracting. If delivering high levels of expertise in key areas is the primary goal, then outsourcing with a partner that has a depth of experience in that area may be the best option. If the organization is most intent on developing specific internal competencies, those areas may best be developed internally, with perhaps some logistical areas being outsourced, as Dow Chemical has done with Delta College Corporate Services (see chapter 5). Clearly, each scenario will be different. But the team will add an important piece to the decision process by weighing carefully the advantages and disadvantages of each scenario it develops.

Select Activities or Functions to Outsource

With the help of these analyses, the team has the information needed to select which activities or functions should be outsourced. As indicated in chapter 1, this is not an all-or-nothing decision. There are multiple outsourcing options: an entire function (such as education and training or information systems); one or many functions (course development, registration, instructor selection); one or more content areas (sales training, quality, or managerial skills); or some combination of these.

As with the other stages in the outsourcing decision process, it is important at this point to keep the goals and the business case, as well as the criteria, before the team. These provide the context in which the team can address issues and concerns, yet focus on finding solutions that meet the objectives.

Learning: Addressing Fears

At this point, when the team is moving from theory and analysis to the reality of making the crucial decisions about which areas to outsource, fears often resurface. In addition to the personal fears at the prospect of losing job(s), the biggest organizational concern is the loss of internal control over a function. People who have entered the process at various points now air their differences in perception of how the department contributes

---

> *to the company. As these fears and concerns arise, it is important to con-tinue to acknowledge them and to filter them through the process. They may generate some new ideas. But whether they add to the richness of discus-sion at this point or not, it is far better to deal with them early on, than to allow them to fester and ultimately to undermine outcomes at the end of the decision process.*
>
> *It is also at such times that the rigor of the process becomes important. Often team leaders and many team members can make a fairly sound intu-itive judgment about what areas should be outsourced. When emotions or resistance threaten the decision process, however, the information gleaned from the analytical process is enormously helpful in moving it forward, with the team on board.*

At Dow Chemical, for example, a new goal caused them to reexamine their training and education operation. With a new corporate-wide focus on performance improvement, it became clear to the training department that they needed to dedicate their resources to this content area. This goal was what led them ultimately to a decision to outsource virtually all of the logis-tical areas to Delta College Corporate Services. Delta took on responsibility for scheduling classrooms and meetings; managing registration; acquiring and distributing training materials; and overseeing food services, mainte-nance, and other contracted services.

Corning, too, was faced with a need to refocus its training and education resources on new corporate strategies. Unlike Dow, however, Corning began by transferring its skills courses to CCFL through a phased implementation process. They began with the lowest risk areas—those courses that had no direct bearing on key company strategies. Once a base of experience was established, they added functions including registration, scheduling, and other services. Later, they expanded the partnership so that the vendor took on more and more content area over time.

These two examples are expanded more fully in later chapters. The chap-ters on Quest Diagnostics, Kaiser Permanente, and Compaq also reflect how these other companies chose different avenues to address their organizations' goals. Collectively, these underscore the notion that there is no single right or wrong solution. Rather, through a combination of analysis, creativity, and focus on the desired outcomes, companies can arrive at decisions about which areas to outsource that are uniquely right for their organizations.

Identify Improvement Opportunities

In the process of examining the department's functions and output, the team needs to add another dimension: assessing current performance. Since the desired outcome of the sourcing decision process is a system that meets goals, this is the time to determine which areas need improvement. One tempting solution for problem areas is, of course, to outsource them. Sending a problem out may or may not resolve it, but it certainly does not provide an automatic solution, in most cases. Sometimes, however, an external resource may be the most desirable choice for a number of reasons.

If the team decides to outsource a problem area, then the supplier needs to understand its customer's needs and requirements very clearly. Unless the team provides information about both the current situation and the desired improvements, the external supplier might reasonably expect to try to match the existing model. If the current model is flawed or broken, matching it leads directly to disappointment or disaster. A clear statement of needed improvements will help the supplier to grasp expectations and will form the basis for both supplier and customer to judge outcomes and manage performance.

Sometimes outsourcing may not be the best solution to fixing problems. The desire to dispatch all trouble could easily send a company down multiple detours from its main focus. Such an impulse will sometimes yield a hodge-podge of disparate little projects rather than a clean, smoothly functioning training system.

Ideally, the outsourcing decision process is accompanied by an assessment of what internal functions can benefit from a process-improvement effort. If, for example, the current registration system yields class lists that routinely include several errors, one solution may be to review the registration process, determine where the errors occur, and fix the problem internally rather than seek a new registration resource. This would certainly be the best decision if the problems occurred in limited areas that could be permanently fixed by one or two simple process changes. On the other hand, a close analysis might disclose that the whole system is based on yesterday's computer system. In such a case, a substantial capital investment as well as changes in personnel might be required to create a system that solves today's problems and provides an appropriate system for the future. In such a case, finding the right external supplier might be the ideal solution.

Regardless of whether an area is to be handled internally or externally, this is the time to identify needs and opportunities for improvement and begin to create improvement plans for at least those areas where the current system is seriously broken. These plans should incorporate a baseline of current practice and should outline the next steps, whether these are undertaken in-house or by a vendor.

Set Baseline Measures

Whether or not a need for improvement is identified, establishing measures and quantifying change are critical aspects of the outsourcing process. These are key tenets of quality. Anecdotes may be entertaining, but they do not provide compelling information on which to base business decisions. Thus the team should establish measures for performance. The place to begin is with baseline data on current practices, so that future change can be accurately quantified. Certainly in the case of outsourcing, both partners need not only to agree upon goals but also to understand where they are starting. The measures should be designed or selected for their value as long-term indicators of progress toward the agreed-upon goals.

In cases where an improvement need is identified, creating an improvement plan is relatively simple if there is a history of ongoing measurement. If no such history exists, it should be initiated immediately. In such a case, there may be real value in involving an outsourcing partner early on. Training firms are likely to have utilized various measures with other customers over time, and they may be able to reduce the time spent reinventing existing tools. They may already have measurement tools or systems that can be either used as is or easily adapted. Experienced training firms are also likely to have some insight into other issues that may affect the measures.

The discussions surrounding goals and measures lay the groundwork for the contract that will eventually be developed. Ultimately, measures provide both clear expectations of what is to be accomplished and a means of determining success—critical elements to the successful long-term management of outsourcing relationships.

Step 3: Choose Vendor(s)

How does the team choose a vendor? Once the team has analyzed its current operations and future needs and pinpointed prime candidates for outsourcing, its next step is to decide who can deliver the service best. This step provides a process for identifying and evaluating prospective vendors in order to make a selection.

As with deciding what to outsource and what to keep, a rich matrix is needed—one that includes such criteria as stability, reputation, financial strength, and cultural fit. The reason for including such characteristics is tied to the philosophy behind outsourcing. Broad-reaching outsourcing plans can enable companies to invest in their core businesses. They do so by outsourcing areas that are *not* their training organization's key strategic services or core competencies to vendors for whom those same areas *are* their core business—their areas of expertise. Ideally, this arrangement will build in the flexibility to anticipate and address future shifts in needs and priorities. Thus the selection of a vendor has implications not just for today, but for tomorrow, and for the changes in both the internal and external environment.

The following four-phase process is recommended for this all-important selection procedure:

- Establish selection criteria.
- Identify potential service providers.
- Analyze capabilities (by using a request for proposal).
- Make tentative decision.

Establish Selection Criteria

There is no magic formula for establishing the criteria against which to assess potential vendors. Some will focus on commonsense issues typically used for most purchasing or sourcing choices, while others are linked to particular needs that have been identified. As in the other outsourcing decision steps, these criteria need to refer back to the business case and overall goals for undertaking this process.

There are two key principles here: (1) Apply the criteria uniformly to all vendors for a fair and accurate assessment; and (2) weight the criteria to reflect the priorities. A grid such as that shown in table 2.4 can be a useful tool in clarifying and prioritizing the criteria and then ensuring that the suppliers are assessed uniformly. The following broad criteria are likely to be on the list for consideration: cost, quality, capabilities, customer service, stability, experience, shared values, and cultural fit. Most of these are standard when it comes to measuring potential vendors, even for contracted services. Cost, quality, and capability are almost always factors, even when other issues are a higher priority. Still, they should not be the only measures, particularly if the desired outcome is an arrangement more like a partnership than like the

Table 2.4. Comparison of Suppliers				
Criteria	Weight	Supplier A	Supplier B	Supplier C
Cost				
Quality				
Capabilities				
Stability				
Experience				
Shared Values				
Cultural Fit				
Other (distance learning capability, industry expertise, implementation in 6 months)				

typical supplier-customer model. Therefore, the criteria must be selected according to how well they reinforce the overall purpose.

Identify Potential Service Providers

Once the team has completed—or nearly completed—defining its selection criteria, team members can begin the search for potential providers. Several resources can be useful in this process.

The first is colleagues in other area companies that have outsourced all or part of their training. They may be partnering with regional suppliers whose capabilities fall in the range of the established criteria. In addition, it never hurts to simply cold call local firms that advertise themselves as training providers. Contacts made through regional chapters of professional human resources organizations can be supplemented with directories from the local Chambers of Commerce or even the Yellow Pages.

Looking locally confers some distinct advantages. First, it is likely that team members have already-established relationships with local colleagues who are willing to share their experiences. Second, it is easier and cheaper to continue probing for additional information in a local setting where each new set of questions can be answered by a short drive, rather than a plane ticket. In such a situation, it is often possible not only to query both sides of the partnership but also to witness it in action. Third, using a local provider—*if the right match exists*—can make building and maintaining the partnership easier over the long term.

In many areas, however—even those with large cities and multiple vendors—the right local partner simply may not exist. Since it is far more important to develop a partnership that works well over the long term than to use a local firm, team members should not be deterred from searching nationally or even internationally to identify prospective partners. The Web sites and publications of professional training, education, and development associations can provide valuable information regarding potential suppliers. In addition, their national conferences offer the opportunity to learn about others' experiences and meet both vendors and their existing partners face-to-face. Team members also will benefit by embarking on a benchmarking effort, focusing on organizations that have undertaken a training partnership similar in scope to the one proposed. Identifying partnerships that are working well can be facilitated by searching the professional journals and published conference proceedings for case studies.

For the long term, it makes sense to choose a reliable firm that has both fiscal and managerial stability. Sometimes a vendor's reputation speaks to these qualities, but it is wise to beware of packaged images and dated reputations. When the team creates the request for proposal (RFP), it should ask vendors to include a client list—not just a list of references—and then check with others who currently work with, or have in the past worked with, the potential supplier.

This step can help the team to assess cultural fit, perhaps one of the hardest areas to pin down because it includes a lot of "soft" criteria that involve values and feelings. These values and feelings translate to behaviors, however, so some observable conduct provides a place to begin an analysis of cultural fit. Vendors also make their own assessments of cultural fit with prospective customers. In fact, this issue is sometimes the critical factor in decisions not to form partnerships, even when all the other elements on the grid looked good.

How does one company learn about another's culture? There may be official company statements about organizational values. While these may be helpful, it is also wise to listen to what people say about the "party line." As with many situations, the gap between the ideal and the real may be anywhere between a crack and a canyon. Investing time on site and talking with a variety of people can have real payback.

Cultural fit usually comes down to the following issues: conception of customer service, problem-solving approach, communication styles, conception and execution of meetings, commitments, and people strategies.

Communication styles, for example, vary greatly. Are employees confrontational or polite? Even something as simple as how loud people talk is an indication of the company's culture: manufacturing employees may speak louder than corporate staff, for example.

When analyzing cultural fit, it may prove helpful to ask the following questions:

- *Conception of Customer Service.* How do they define *customers,* and what standards do they set and consistently meet in dealing with them? Do they work hard at understanding and meeting customer requirements? Do they redefine customer problems in terms of their own particular bias or expertise? Are they sensitive to, and respectful of, differences?

- *Problem-solving Approach.* How do they identify and solve problems? Do they collaborate with their customers and with one another? Do they send in an expert or a "heavy"? Do they pretend problems do not exist?

- *Communication Styles.* How do the people in the organization talk to one another? Are they polite, blunt, open, caring, rude? Does the organization focus on improving listening and communication skills, or are these put aside in favor of spending the company's energy on "real" business issues?

- *Conception and Execution of Meetings.* What is the organization's concept of a good meeting? Do they assemble people and hand down decisions? Do they discuss issues openly? Do they meet for the sake of meeting? Do they have a purpose, an agenda, and a process that is used consistently?

- *Corporate Commitments.* What things are they most strongly committed to? Does "meeting a deadline" mean having it on the desk the day before; delivering sometime within the week; renegotiating for more time as other needs arise? Where does price come in? Do they feel free to change after they have made a commitment to a customer; live by the quote no matter what; renegotiate based on quantifiable changes?

- *People Strategies.* How do they select and manage their people? Do they seek the best or a minimum standard? Do they have processes in place for getting to know prospective employees and following their progress? Do they have a performance management system that includes setting goals and providing resources to help employees and contractors achieve them? How do they reward success?

Beyond the culture questions listed above, there may be others that are important in deciding whether a relationship will work. Teams should use all their powers of observation to pick up on ways that their organization fits with a particular supplier—or does not fit. It is difficult but important to try to identify trade-offs. What differing attitudes and behaviors can an organization live with if they see certain others that strike them as important? What unique features and capabilities set one vendor apart from another? Compaq Computer, for example, both sought and recognized Training & Development Systems's (TDS) real strength in management of training delivery and logistics. Sometimes expertise in the company's industry is critical for the training function, and sometimes a company searches for a vendor that is knowledgeable about the company itself.

Just as it is important for companies to assess prospective vendors, it is equally critical for suppliers to do their own assessment. Companies and vendors may reach different conclusions about their prospective partnership. Sometimes those differing perceptions lead to healthy discussions about how they would work through their differences. On occasion, however, they will persuade a potential partner to walk away from a contract because they think the two cultures are sufficiently different that the project would ultimately fail.

Analyze Capabilities

Having defined, identified, and prioritized the criteria for a partner *and developed a list of potential service providers,* the team can then gather the information it needs to assess potential vendors. A company uses an RFP to communicate its requirements to possible vendors, and thus defines how they will be measured. The RFP introduces the company, its background and goals, its culture and values, and its specific needs. This document also asks for parallel information from the vendor. In particular, the RFP asks the vendor to explain its capabilities for providing the needed services, at what cost, and at what level of quality. The RFP reflects the criteria the team has developed, and it builds in ways to assess how each prospective supplier measures up in each area.

In late 1995, Kaiser Permanente (KP) developed a particularly thoughtful and thorough RFP. It includes a three-paragraph description of their company, along with a page on the organization's vision and expectations for a strategic alliance with a training partner. Having established this very important context up front, the RFP then outlines a description of needs, vendor qualifications, and a request for specific examples of how the prospective vendor has met KP's expectations. Finally, it asks some open-ended questions that address the vendors' views on their compatibility with KP. The whole document has an air of candor and makes it clear that the chosen vendor will be invited and expected to share in solving problems and achieving KP's organizational vision. Statements like the following characterize the RFP: "We want a partner who believes in learning, who knows about the possibilities AND the limitations of traditional training approaches, and who guarantees service AND outcomes." The proposals KP received gave them a wealth of information in a format that was consistent from one supplier to another and yet consumed little of their time to digest. It provided a very real platform from which to take the next steps in analyzing the capabilities of prospective vendors.

Once the company receives the proposal, the next step is to clarify issues that arise from it. Beyond this, it is important to have discussions—at least some of which should be face-to-face—in which the company and the prospective vendor explore together in greater depth how they would work together. Another of these steps is talking with suppliers' current and past customers. The team needs to find out what has worked well, what has not, how progress has been made, and how issues have been resolved. It is particularly important to probe areas that are especially significant for the company and to recognize where differences between cultures may have led to appropriately different structures and systems. The RFP and follow-up conversations should make it possible for the team not only to fill in the charts comparing prospective suppliers with quantitative information but also to gain a deeper, qualitative understanding of each organization.

Make Tentative Decision

For the list of criteria to be useful now that there is a list of potential players, the team needs a system of analysis that enables comparison of each potential vendor with the others. In *The New Rational Manager* (1981),

Charles H. Kepner and Benjamin B. Tregoe describe a practical, straightforward decision-making process. First, they divide the criteria into "musts" and "wants." The musts are definable into either/or categories. In a hypothetical example, one must might be for the vendors to have technical support sufficient to handle 120,000 registrations per month. The first round of analysis measures the vendors against this: Do they have this capacity or not? Those that do not are no longer considered.

The wants are those relative measures that are important but cannot be quantified into yes or no answers. Taking the registration technology example again, perhaps the company wants to increase the quantity of training and education provided, and is therefore looking for a supplier with a strong commitment to leading-edge technology that would enable it to keep pace with the company's projected growth. In such a case, the company would look for the vendor that shows this commitment *more than the others.* In such a situation, the team's assessment would be qualitative rather than binary. The question would become: Who is the best?

This is where a weighted comparison of suppliers can be useful (see table 2.5). This tool provides a structure for identifying those wants that have the highest value and for weighting them accordingly. By giving careful consideration of the weights in relation to the company's goals for outsourcing, the team arrives at a numeric reflection of how well each vendor meets the outsourcing goals, rather than simply an objective but perhaps irrelevant evaluation of these vendors.

Table 2.5 has been expanded and filled in, and the next steps taken to create a weighted analysis of the company's wants. The suppliers that make it to this cut are those that have already passed the "must" screening. This tool helps to force healthy discussion about priorities and then to understand how well each supplier may be able to meet them.

The priority weights in the second column reflect that distance learning capability is the company's highest priority, and six-month implementation the lowest. Suppliers are scored on each criterion on a scale of 1–10. From this tool, it would appear that suppliers A and C are very close, and both are preferable to supplier B.

As tidy as the information appears in such a format, however, the outsourcing decision process is neither entirely quantitative nor entirely linear. Once the critical information is in and analyzed, it is healthy to circle back and check on things that do not feel right. Instinct can be an important ally in

Table 2.5. Weighted Comparison of Suppliers

"Want" Criteria	Priority Weight	Supplier A		Supplier B		Supplier C	
		Score	Weight	Score	Weight	Score	Weight
Distance learning capability	10	8	80	7	70	10	100
Industry expertise	9	10	90	9	81	9	81
Implements in 6 months	8	10	80	7	56	8	64
Totals			250		207		245

the decision process. It is equally important, however, not to allow the whole process to be undermined or scuttled for the wrong reasons. Once the team has quantified the prospective vendors' capabilities, it has the basis for a tentative decision.

Step 4: Contract with Vendor

What is involved in contracting an outsourcing alliance? The contract is a necessary document. It forms the legal agreement between the company and its outsourcing supplier. It establishes guidelines for working together and addresses a number of specific issues. It also spells out a way for the organizations to part ways if things do not work out.

Essentially, the contract addresses the fundamental contradiction at the heart of any outsourcing arrangement. The two contracting parties are partners and allies in delivering services and in seeking to win customer satisfaction. But the supplier wants to maximize profits, while the customer wants to minimize costs. The supplier also wants to minimize risks or commitments, while the customer wants to maximize the promise of reliable performance. The hope is that the contract holds these elements in creative tension to the benefit of both parties. But it can do so only if it is seen as a reflection of the work that has already been done by both parties and their intentions for the future of their relationship. This typically will not happen if the contracting process is handed off to the legal department in isolation from the team.

There are nearly as many different approaches to contracting as there are companies. Companies and their suppliers should create a contract that is a brief written expression of a profound understanding between two organizations.

The following set of actions will build a platform for a lasting architecture, balance these forces, and to pave the way for future success:

- Set goals and performance measures.
- Decide exactly what will be negotiated.
- Determine the process for changing requirements.

Set Goals and Performance Measures

Before entering into contract negotiations, the team needs to benchmark the systems it proposes to outsource and establish baseline measures, as discussed in Step 2. What is written into the contract should be an expression of homework already done—of goals that both parties agree to, based on appropriate measures with real baseline data.

Example: Baseline Data

In a meeting where the contract was already being negotiated, a vendor's computer person identified the prospective customer's system as a standard package. On this basis, she was convinced that her company would be able to take over their registration rather easily. The systems were compatible. In good faith, the customer's vice president agreed, but one of their team members noted quietly, "It is not going to work." Once the project got off the ground, it turned out their computer system did not work. They were slipping people into courses by hand whenever necessary. Their team member knew the reality, but the vendor failed to follow through and probe more deeply. They needed to go below the surface and analyze the customer's system thoroughly—to acquire baseline data on all important criteria—long before they got to the point of writing a contract. Needless to say, it was a costly lesson.

This example reflects the importance of gathering baseline data at a level of detail that is sufficient to provide an accurate reflection of a system. One learning from this situation was that the existing system should have been identified as an improvement opportunity. With sufficient information, either the customer or the vendor might have been able to fix the broken system. But without having identified that need, the partners begin their relationship with a strike against future success. Such problems are not insurmountable, but they are avoidable—and that is infinitely preferable.

Decide What to Negotiate

In a paper delivered at a conference in 1997, John Branning of J.B. Stevens Associates recommends these items for negotiation: data rights, penalties, payment schedules, fee structure, and schedule of deliveries. They recommend that the contract terms and conditions specified include the following: a description of services, terms of agreement, compensation, inspection and acceptance, termination for convenience, termination for default, post-termination transition, dispute resolution, right of access, confidential information, limitation of liability, pricing, and other miscellaneous items that may be important to either party. There is a lot of wisdom and experience behind their recommendations—and a lot of room for interpretation within them.

The system of agreements employed by one major training and education supplier takes the elements that Branning outlines into account, but they have found that the really important elements of contracting are understanding and trust. Without these, the document simply entitles the partners to endless wrangling. This is not to suggest, however, that partners can afford for the terms of their contract to be hazy. They cannot. Thus this supplier enters into negotiations with a clear understanding of what they will negotiate and what they will not and have found that their partners do exactly the same. By insisting on very clear statements of expectation in the contract, they have precluded misunderstandings and shored up the feeling of mutual trust.

Example: Contract Error

A large company contracted with a provider for a major portion of its training. The training firm negotiated a clause giving them exclusive rights to do all of the new training work that might develop over the period of the contract. Unfortunately the company failed to negotiate any pricing conditions relative to this new work. What happened? The fees for new training programs—important new initiatives—were off the charts. The "ouch" was not only for the customer, it was also for the supplier. Because each party had different expectations that were not negotiated up front, the relationship fell apart. There were bad feelings, and equally important, a loss of

---

(Example: Contract Error *continued*)

both parties' investment of time and credibility. Now the company had to start over, and the supplier lost both a potentially very good customer and some degree of reputation in the training industry.

This example reveals why it is important to decide what will be negotiated and then follow through. It deals with pricing, but similar problems have arisen over other fundamentals such as delivery schedules and quality. Why do such difficulties arise? In part, they occur because it is impossible for each partner to know everything about the other, or to anticipate what lies ahead. Although there are never any guarantees, the surest way to preclude problems is by a very thorough process up front, and a very thorough and careful delineation of expectations not only for the present but also for the future.

One final specific element to be negotiated is the length of the contract period. A three- to four-year contract, with the option for rolling renewals, seems to work best. At the end of each year, the contract is renegotiated for the next three years. The rationale for this recommendation is that a real partnership is too extensive for any shorter time frame. Within this framework, however, a six-month review is needed, along with an escape clause. If the relationship is not working and is clearly not going to work, both parties should agree to dissolve the partnership as soon as possible. So the first six months should be seen as a trial period. The worst horror stories about outsourcing involve long and binding contracts in which a party is stuck in a relationship that has proved too costly, too complicated, or sometimes both. The rationale for creating a rolling renewal option is that the partnership maintains its long-term focus and momentum. It precludes the stop-and-start mentality that occurs as partners reach the end of a three-year contract and begin to ask, "Now what?" With a rolling renewal, the plan is already in place and up-to-date.

Determine Process for Changing Requirements

Nearly every outsourcing arrangement falls into the same dilemma: In the beginning, the firm decides to outsource six items, but often even before the ink on the contract is dry, it becomes clear that it makes sense to add two or three more things to the list. And, when the relationship is working well, that will probably continue to happen. Contracts always involve a trade-off: the tighter the contract, the less flexibility, but also the less trouble experienced in getting immediate requirements met. Still, for many outsourcing arrangements, there have been difficulties with long-term contracts, particularly for those areas that are heavily linked to technology. Part of the contract should spell out how such changes should be dealt with.

If a firm wants a relationship that basically keeps the decision making internal and hands the execution over to the vendor, then the contract needs to spell that out. The contract sets forth this fundamental principal of how future change will occur. It may be tempting to write a loose "relational" partnership into the contract, but it is more important to be sure that the expectations and the agreement match. Assumptions about transparency, communications, roles and responsibilities, and other important "soft" aspects of how the partners will work together need to be addressed before negotiations begin. Once agreed upon, they need to be expressed in a contract.

Similarly, building in a periodic review of the entire contract and relationship helps ensure that it works for both parties. This is especially important given the flux of the market and how frequently and substantively corporations shift and restructure. As is revealed in chapter 4, Quest Diagnostics began life as a spin-off from Corning, which brought together under one umbrella a number of discrete smaller firms. When the relationship with its training partner began, Quest was convinced that they needed an open workshop system. Within three months of the start-up of the partnership, however, Quest underwent a series of corporate change initiatives. The implications for the supplier were profound: They were now to design, develop, and deliver training—very different from the initial expectations both partners had. Fortunately, the contract built in a process that allowed the partners to meet changing requirements.

Step 5: Transition

What is needed in order to make the transition work? Every change—from personal rites of passage like leaving home or getting married to organizational restructuring or outsourcing—involves a transition. During this in-between time, things certainly are not what they used to be, but they are not yet what they are going to be either. The good news is that, in an organization, this unsettled—and unsettling—period of time can be mapped and managed. Transitions are generally smoother when they are planned as complete processes, including periodic feedback and adjustment. Formalizing a plan for the transition reaps benefits not only in moving the process forward but also in creating an atmosphere of calm. The plan becomes a reality by virtue of the people who oversee, manage, and communicate it.

A key part of the transition planning process is communicating broadly and clearly both the transition plan and progress against it. The objective of this effort is to ensure that everyone affected knows where things stand and what is coming. This not only helps to keep the process on track and moving along, it also helps to create confidence in the new reality and thus alleviate some of the inevitable malaise that accompanies any major change. Information is an important antidote to fear and anxiety. Some companies create a special team dedicated to the transition process—and particularly to communicating about it—while others set up the new configuration but outline policies and procedures that specifically address the needs of the in-between time.

No matter what format the company chooses to adopt, the following five activities should be included in the transition planning process:

- Create a specific project plan for the transition.
- Develop a people strategy.
- Develop a trust strategy.
- Define decision diamonds.
- Implement.

Create a Transition Project Plan

The transition project plan maps out the order of change, the time needed for each phase, and the key players. It should include all of the elements of any other project plan: a list of actions correlated to objectives, timeline, milestones and measures, and roles and responsibilities. Table 2.6 shows these basic elements of the project plan in simplified form. Such a plan builds in

Table 2.6. Transition Project Plan					
Phase	Objectives	Actions	Deadlines	Milestones and Measures	Responsibility

requirements for review, and thereby opportunities to change course, as needed.

The transfer of responsibilities for outsourcing should always be phased, much like a pilot program. For example, the first phase might consist of migrating the first 10 courses, followed by an assessment using milestones and measures established in advance, as well as being alert for any new learnings. This will provide the basis for deciding what changes might need to be made to the plan.

An important aspect of the transition planning process is anticipating what might go wrong. Once again, in *The New Rational Manager* (page 142), Kepner and Tregoe offer a valuable process: potential problem analysis (PPA). This analysis requires an instinct for posing questions that are sometimes unwelcome: What could go wrong? and What can we do about it now? The payback, however, can be the prevention of glitches, or even catastrophes. Kepner and Tregoe define four activities in PPA:

> *Identification of vulnerable areas* of an undertaking, project, operation, event, plan, etc.
>
> *Identification of specific potential problems* within these vulnerable areas that could have sufficient negative effect on the operation to merit taking action now.
>
> *Identification of the likely causes* of these potential problems and *identification of actions to prevent* them from occurring.
>
> *Identification of contingent actions* that can be taken if preventive actions fail, or where no preventive action is possible.

As the authors point out, the techniques of PPA are few and easy to understand; learning to use them well can take 20 years. But even an inexperienced team can benefit by applying the concepts of PPA to their transition planning process.

Another useful approach to the transition step is to define responsibilities and roles. In *Managing Transitions: Making the Most of Change* (1991), William Bridges suggests using an interim group to guide the transition. These seven to 12 people form a special transition monitoring team (TMT) that meets weekly to check on how the process is going. It is not an existing group, but one formed of representatives of a wide range of stakeholders. This means that it will answer to the outsourcing team. The TMT members keep their fingers on the pulse as everyone adjusts to the new arrangement. They do not make decisions, but instead provide a locus for the rumor mill, serve as a focus group to test new initiatives, and foster communications in several directions.

The more critical role, and the one that often defines the success of the venture over the long haul, is the partnership manager. Both parties need someone who is the crucial liaison between the organizations. Some have questioned whether this role is needed, but with so many issues in a constantly changing relationship, it is critical. This role will be discussed more in Step 6: Manage and Improve.

Develop a People Strategy

As soon as the new outsourcing structure and responsibilities are outlined, the appropriate manager(s) need to frame a long-term work plan. What tasks will need to be performed under the new plan, and what kinds of skills and talents will they require? Once rough job descriptions and requirements are outlined—often involving new positions for the outsourcing supplier as well as the customer—the next step is to look for the best people to fill them.

As these decisions are being made, another important aspect of ensuring success is planning for the development of employees who remain with the company. Certainly there will be a need to review the background, experience, and skills of all employees in relation to the new roles they will fill and plan the means for them to meet the new needs successfully. In addition, there is likely to be an immediate need to help employees develop skill in, and knowledge about, how to work in a collaborative environment where responsibilities may be shared—sometimes with strangers. Planning to help employees through this transition is one way to help ensure the success of outsourcing. And although planning for such change is not easy, it is far less draining than planning for the exodus of valued employees.

One of the most difficult things to recognize and address is the likelihood that there will be no match between new jobs and existing employees in some situations. Especially in these circumstances, where perhaps long-term employees appear to have no place in the new organization, it is critical to keep the goals of the project in sight and make the best selection decisions to ensure success. At the same time, it is important to provide as much assistance as the company allows in helping the affected employee(s) find other positions within the company or new positions outside—and to show compassion.

Each company is likely to have its own policy and procedures for how downsizing is handled. If this is the first outsourcing to occur in the company, it may be time to revisit those procedures and adapt or revolutionize them, as needed. Developing an overall strategy at the outset precludes a piecemeal, case-by-case approach. At Corning, three options were developed: remain within the education and training department, find another position within the company, or go through outplacement. In the last option, the company provided services to help the former employee either find another position or establish his or her own consulting firm.

Certainly outsourcing is a situation in which some employees may very well wind up performing essentially the same jobs as before, but under the auspices of a different organization. In this case, both organizations need to look at all of the aspects of employment—reporting structure, salary, benefits, policies, location—and anticipate where the transitions may be difficult. Despite all of the best planning and the best intentions, of course, there will be resistance. This is more than an individual issue; typically such decisions affect the fabric of the workplace, at least in the short term. This underscores once again the need for planning the transition, including a people strategy.

Learning: People Strategy

*Some ill-feeling is natural. People really are losing something. They might be sad about their individual loss, anxious about what is expected from them in a changed role, fearful about additional future changes, or angry about the whole complex change. Simply recognizing these feelings goes a long way in building morale, far more than brightly trumpeting the benefits of the outsourcing venture. While people might understand those benefits intellectually, particularly if other functions in the company currently outsource, they might not **feel** it. Ill-feelings are one thing, but anger that gets channeled into counterproductive behavior must be avoided. A sound people strategy distinguishes appropriate feelings from inappropriate actions.*

To identify potential sources of resistance, William Bridges begins by asking, "Who's losing what?" Among the issues employees face are losing workmates, work locations, beneficial relationships with superiors, familiar ways of doing things, control, and other turf issues. All are potential sore points. Bridges notes, however, that some may be more elusive, such as losing a sense of the company's character and values. In situations where firms laid off employees for the first time, for instance, often it was not the actual decision to eliminate particular jobs, but the loss of a long-standing commitment that caused ill-feeling.

The most effective strategy for addressing ill-feelings and resistance is clear, consistent, repeated, honest, two-way communication. Such communication must be planned and managed; it does not just happen. In the absence of information, rumors and misinformation flourish. People fill in the gaps, and what gets circulated is often counterproductive. The communication plan should include the following key elements:

- speed in getting out what is known and decided as soon as it is known
- repetition of the rationale: why outsourcing is the right business decision
- an outline of the plan elements, with time frames and clear indications of the current status in relation to the plan
- multiple means and consistent messages: memos, voice messages, newsletters, posters, and so forth
- face-to-face meetings, including opportunities for two-way communication: presentations, meetings, and more informal but equally deliberate conversations
- honest answers that reflect respect for employees and their concerns

Bridges notes that decision makers are often reluctant to communicate. They say, "It's not all decided yet," or, "We told them once." This reluctance must be overcome by the stronger rationale for allaying fears and putting the rumor mill out of business before it picks up speed and efficiency. This is where a TMT can be beneficial. Such a team can be charged with not only communicating messages but also listening for what is being said. Not all comments need to be answered formally, but people do need assurance that they are being heard. Commissioning a group of designated listeners is one strategy to achieve this.

Develop a Trust Strategy

While the strategy for dealing with people is often an internal effort, building trust is both internal and external. It may seem obvious, but it is worth a reminder: Trust is built on honoring commitments and telling the truth consistently, over time. It is reflected in how both parties write the contract, and even more so in how they develop their working relationships.

Building trust begins with a fundamental question: How much trust do you want? One model is relatively rigid, but has predictable outcomes based on strict adherence to the contract. Such an arrangement requires that this document outline virtually every detail and contingency of how the partners will work together. Once the contract is written, the ongoing communications, monitoring, and management strategies also need to adhere to the letter of the document. In such a model, there is little possibility for failure, but the restrictions imposed limit exciting possibilities that may arise in a more collaborative arrangement.

Another model is a more flexible relationship that not only fulfills the contractual agreement but also enables the kind of risk taking that a manager might encourage within his or her own firm. This type of arrangement requires building a level of credibility well beyond the details of the contract. It depends on much more open communications as well as shared planning and problem solving. It is riskier but has the potential benefits associated with people coming together in a real synergy. Fortunately, the risks of such a relationship can be minimized.

In a paper entitled "Partners in Quality" delivered at a conference in 1991, the Atlanta Consulting Group points out that trust in the corporate partnership is built on a foundation of previous actions. First, mutual agreements are negotiated, then fulfilled, or worked out in mutually beneficial ways if they cannot be kept. If this were a traditional vendor-supplier relationship, that would be all that was necessary. But in the new business arrangements, partners need to go further. Fulfilling contractual agreements builds each party's credibility, and that credibility fosters open communication. Guarded and miserly control of information serves only to shut down the relationship, squelching creative approaches that could lead to opportunities. But the greatest danger is that a tight grip on information corrodes the relationship until even necessary feedback and warnings are only hesitantly offered. To avoid this, the Atlanta Consulting Group offers several specific strategies for building trust: initiate, collaborate, provide/solicit, and make and keep agreements.

In the start-up of a new outsourcing relationship, problems can be identified and addressed constructively, or they can be seen as signs that the process is not working and will never work. For the best chance at success, both partners must take 100 percent responsibility for the success of the venture.

Atlanta calls this strategy "initiate," where both sides have an ongoing commitment to offer improvements to specific tasks and the relationship. As a result, simply recognizing problems—and particularly laying blame for them—are not rewarded, whereas finding solutions and strengthening the partnership have real payoffs for the individual employee as well as for the partnership.

Example: Taking Responsibility

At Corning, all affected employees wrote this sentence into their performance objectives, "I take responsibility for the success of the project." This helped to focus the employees' attitudes and actions on positive, problem-solving approaches, and certainly played a part in growing a very successful partnership.

The second component is "collaborate," a strategy that is both internal and external. Collaboration means that people shift how they think about the relationship, emphasizing the mutual benefits. This requires setting up communications, working teams, and other structures that continually orient this win-win arrangement toward a common goal.

One specific communication strategy is what Atlanta calls "provide/solicit." Both customer and supplier agree to ensure that everyone has the information needed to make the whole program work. Disaster looms every time the relationship telescopes to the point at which only the partnership manager feeds information. Too much filtering, a sure sign of control issues (and by extension a trust problem), means that not all the information needed is being supplied. A process must be in place to solicit the kind and amount of information needed, in which all parties know it will be forthcoming. This process, of course, must go both ways.

Example: Working Together

Corning and CCFL developed a strategy for working together that was designed to build trust, as well as to achieve results. They agreed to—and followed through on—documenting processes, establishing common key results indicators (KRIs), meeting together regularly, and celebrating successes together. As they shared these experiences, their trust in one another grew and formed the foundation for a very successful partnership.

Finally, as the relationship continues, credibility is enhanced and trust built as further agreements are made and fulfilled. "Make and keep agreements" is the fourth element of trust building that Atlanta advocates. As problems arise or as the business climate shifts, the partners can cement their relationship and get the job done well by making clear, specific, achievable agreements that deal with the situation in a mutually beneficial way. As discussed in chapter 5, Dow and Delta applied this principle, working through major organizational shifts, each time reevaluating their agreements, responsibilities, and roles, and each time coming to a stronger sense of trust.

Define Decision Diamonds

In Step 1, points of evaluation and decision were identified and used in the decision-making process. Now it is important to define them for the outsourcing transition plan. Of all the stages in outsourcing, the transition may be the one in which the decision diamonds are most crucial. The transition project plan outlines the tasks in sequence. As that plan is being developed, the team needs to anticipate and build in the points at which it will need to make decisions. Equally important, it needs to lay the groundwork—the means of checking the environment for change, touching base with the sponsor, and synthesizing information that is required in the decision diamond process (see figure 2.1).

Primarily, though, key decisions are correlated to the measures of success. One way of determining critical decision points is to review these measures and use them as a logical framework around which to build the decision diamonds. For instance, the first phase of the transition might be to migrate the first set of courses to the supplier. Before this phase is implemented, the team establishes goals and measures of success, with the agreement of the supplier. The completion of the first set of courses, and the collection of data from them, poses a logical place to review performance against the goals and measures. This also provides a natural opportunity for a decision diamond.

If this expectation has been built in and communicated from the beginning, it is likely to be a positive experience. Both partners will be prepared to contribute information, ideas, and insights to the benefit of future collaborative efforts. If it is a disaster, the whole enterprise can be called to a halt. If there are serious problems, these can be addressed and resolved before moving on. If all is working even better than expected, the migration of programs can be affirmed or perhaps even accelerated. In most cases, however, this decision diamond provides an opportunity to learn what went well and what did not, and to make plans for improvement. Adding in this checkpoint with the sponsor, a scan for changes in the environment, and a summary of information creates a sound basis on which to determine and communicate clear next steps. Thus the decision diamond acts as an important element in an iterative, continuous improvement process.

There are certain to be areas where planning the decision points is less obvious than at the end of a set of courses. Transitioning to a new registration system might be one of those. In such a circumstance, it will be important for the partners to divide that major undertaking into smaller process steps, with milestones and measures built in for each. In the planning process, the team will need to look for the points at which it should logically make the decision to move ahead or call a halt.

Another aspect of planning is to have a crisis plan in place. If the registration process suddenly yields strange information, an instructor contracted for the next 12 months proves to be utterly unreliable, the heating plant crashes in the main training facility, or some other disaster occurs, the rescue can occur much more successfully if there is a crisis plan in place. Such a plan should include the means for gathering the necessary facts, marshalling the team of decision makers, and doing whatever is necessary to move ahead or stop instantly, before further damage is done.

Implement

This is the part that seems obvious and always proves more difficult and time consuming than anyone ever imagines. Here is where the project plan really pays off, where trust is a must, where communications are hard and take up way too much time but are more important than ever. Guiding the implementation requires the patience of Job and the humor of Robin Williams. Most people see the transition as the place where things might fall apart. Fortunately, this in-between time also holds tremendous opportunities that may not have been mapped out earlier. Good planning needs to be supplemented by wise management in order to prevent the worst and take advantage of the best.

Step 6: Manage and Improve

What are the critical elements in managing outsourcing for long-term success? One of the goals of outsourcing, as of any business venture, is continual improvement. As noted throughout this chapter, however, an outsourcing partnership incorporates some unique circumstances. These demand some distinct differences in the particular people chosen to manage the relationship as well as in the ways that they manage, monitor, and improve the output of the blended organizations.

The challenges that are somewhat unique to the management of outsourcing can be categorized in three ways. The first is a significant additional demand placed on the company's internal management of the partnership. Not only must the company manage its own contact with internal customers for outsourced services—line managers and the users themselves—but it also must ensure similar access for its outsourcing suppliers. The second unique outsourcing management challenge is the supplier's management of its own employees who are housed off site, at the partner's location. The implications of such an arrangement include shared management of these employees in a matrixed environment and dealing with the influences of a different organizational culture. The third outsourcing management challenge is the requirement that both partnership managers learn—and help their employees to learn—a style of working that involves shared decision making.

In addition to these structural managerial differences, there are other differences resulting from the fact of outsourcing. One is the constancy of change—even more change than is found in most other business environments. In outsourcing, there never comes a point at which managers can exclaim with satisfaction, "Well, we've operationalized that!" and move on. Thus the outsourcing situation requires that the managers selected have an unusual degree of flexibility, as well as the ability to hold fast to the factors that are important.

Another factor that decidedly influences the choice of manager and the management approach is the inevitable differences between or among the partnering organizations. As noted earlier, organizations differ in their values, culture, and work styles, as well as in the objectives on which each is focused. In chapter 9, James Shillaber and Alexandra Miller will address the unique challenge of assessing the success of training in an outsourced setting.

Here are some strategies that can help ensure successful long-term partnership management:

- Select and develop the partnership managers.
- Establish and maintain access to line sponsors and company leaders.

- Manage personnel in off-site locations and matrixed reporting structures.
- Reinforce the company's culture.
- Refine the lines and means of communication.
- Transfer knowledge.

Select and Develop Managers

As noted in the Step 5, these "point players" are central to the continual health of this sort of venture. Partnership managers should be selected at the beginning of the transition—or sooner—with the expectation that the process will always need an overseer. The particular challenges that these managers will face over the long term are somewhat different from those that other line managers face.

First, as noted, partnership managers will always operate in an environment of change, or at least an atmosphere that feels more kinetic than most staff-management situations. It is one thing to add responsibilities within a single organization. That happens all the time. For an internal training and education organization, adding a new course or finding a new resource is not unusual. Even redoing a needs assessment in light of new company initiatives is all part of the work fabric. When two or more organizations are joined, however, each of these changes seems magnified. In many cases, advance planning will have provided well-defined processes and roles that accommodate such changes. But sometimes these simply do not exist or do not work as expected. Regardless of these factors, the need for communication is considerably magnified.

Second, natural tensions accrue from the different roles that each manager plays. The company's partnership manager clearly has a vested interest in seeing that the sponsors and other internal customers at a managerial level are satisfied and that costs are held down. The training provider's manager is more likely to focus directly on the satisfaction of the end-user of their services—the student—and to ensure that the arrangement is profitable to his or her firm. Despite how they look on paper, these are not necessarily incompatible goals and interests. The differences do mean that each manager must know how to build and earn trust, stay focused on the goals of the venture, and bring people together to arrive at creative, practical solutions. And then, of course, partnership managers on both sides must address other challenges: the multiple differences in culture, values, work habits, systems, and all the rest.

Selecting a manager who is well equipped to deal with all of these circumstances (and others described below) is absolutely crucial to the success of the venture. This person must have the right combination of leadership and managerial skills and personal traits to maintain the relationship. The ability to maintain a balance between the big picture and the daily details is essential. Other critical characteristics are personal leadership qualities, systematic organizational strengths, strong communication skills and instincts, comfort with change and conflict, skill in negotiation and compromise, and the ability to connect on a personal level with a varied cast of characters. As if those traits were not enough, there is one more: the ability to make it all happen but give the credit for doing so to others.

This blend of capabilities plays out in the varied tasks that come up on a regular basis. For example, it may be necessary to persuade the legal department to write an entirely different kind of contract than they have ever done before (or believe possible); to insist that the security department provide company badges to trainers who are not company employees; and to work out a parking arrangement that keeps company employees happy and still allows trainers to have easy access for hauling their mountain of bags and parcels. The same week may include the monthly operations meeting; a walk through three different sites just to say "Hi" and stay connected with trainers in the field; a planning session for the next phase of the orientation program; a meeting with manufacturing engineers to ferret out the truth behind mounting rumors; and drafting a speech for a senior vice president to give about this unique outsourcing partnership.

Given this atmosphere in which the manager is pulled simultaneously in many directions, as well as the environment of change and the tension between the organizations, it is clear that the outsourcing partnership benefits not only from managers' personal leadership skills but also from their development and implementation of appropriate systems. The venture is much more likely to succeed if the managers clearly define processes and roles, and then adhere to them. This is not to suggest rigidity, but rather a framework for getting the work done as efficiently as possible. Having systems in place reduces the potential for wasting enormous amounts of time in figuring out how to accommodate each new request. Making roles very clear not only helps people to understand what their responsibilities are—and are not—but also helps to minimize turf issues that can so easily arise in these situations.

The realities and special needs described above strongly suggest two things: (1) that the right person be selected for the partnership manager's role; and (2) that this person have the right opportunities to develop or enhance the uniquely important skills demanded by the job. Once in the role, this manager, along with his or her supervisor(s), needs to plan and follow through on appropriate learning opportunities. More than almost any other job, the continually unfolding challenges of this position will require constant growth.

Establish and Maintain Access to Leaders

Seamless and *transparent* are two words often used in describing good outsourcing relationships. Nowhere do seamlessness and transparency matter more than in access to people. It is particularly important for the outsourcing partnership managers, training designers, trainers, systems administrators, and others who contribute to the training process to talk directly with the people who use their services, including line sponsors and company leaders. One important task for the company's partnership manager is to define this access and then be sure it continues to be open. The vendor's partnership manager has the responsibility to ensure that this access is used well.

Nearly every training vendor has at least a few war stories about situations in which their people have been denied access to the direct customers. Almost inevitably, this leads to errors or omissions in the training that is delivered, resulting in unhappy customers. Likewise, some company outsourcing managers can tell tales of nuts-and-bolts meetings where only the vendor's manager showed up (omitting those employees who were directly involved with the customer) and that clearly failed to probe the right areas or communicate the right messages to the actual service providers.

As these examples suggest, trouble is inevitable when the relationship telescopes to the two managers. This is, at its essence, a trust issue. The customer declares that their training people will communicate to the vendor on a need-to-know basis. Meanwhile the vendor gets feedback from workshop participants or from registrants, which might have real value to the customer—but only if shared. Such dilemmas reflect the politics of the situation. The training team wants to control information as a way of protecting and justifying themselves in the face of this outside vendor. Or the training manager has a high need for control and, in meeting this personal need, inadvertently sabotages the success of the project.

In addition to building relationships with the line managers who actually purchase and use the training provided, the managers need to work at building the relationship between the vendors and the company sponsors and leaders who have ultimate decision-making authority over the outsourcing relationship. It is the job of both partnership managers to see that these relationships are built and nurtured over time.

Each company will have its own approach to dealing with external team members. Certainly there need to be systems for regular communications with and among all the people involved. In addition, partners should be encouraged to use all appropriate means to help create seamless relationships. One opportunity may be to involve some or all of the outsourcing suppliers in the customer company's orientation program. In fact, in many outsourcing arrangements, it is the supplier who delivers the orientation, and thus it is a short hop to including their own employees and contractors in the program. Another opportunity may be to invite the training group to department celebrations, picnics, and other informal team-building activities.

Manage Off-Site Personnel

Although it is very important for partners to build those seamless relationships, doing so makes the vendor manager's job a lot tougher. Developing an organization that looks like part of the customer's requires the vendor's manager to develop a well-thought-out management system. This is particularly important—and particularly difficult—when, as often happens, some of the trainers and other staff members are housed at the customer's site.

The paradox is that the very elements that can be most valuable in making the training vendor's employees close to the company are the same elements that make the manager's job very difficult. Having staff at the customer's location is ideal in many ways because it enables them to become a very real part of the company's team. In addition, having trainers report not only to the vendor but also to the line manager of the group where they are delivering training enables them to understand present needs and anticipate future ones. But these conditions mean that the vendor's employee is working away from the employer's location and in a matrixed reporting structure. And guess which manager sees this employee most often? That's right—*not* the employer.

When there are multiple trainers in multiple sites, the job of staying in touch with all of them gets even tougher. The whole situation precludes anything remotely resembling "management by walking around."

In addition, since the training employee reports to a customer's on-site manager and is physically surrounded by the customer's work environment, it is natural for that person to become closer to the customer than to the employer. Under these circumstances, it is not at all unusual for an employee to hear important new information or feedback or to make decisions without ever discussing them with his or her employer. The situation can be compounded when several members of the training organization work at a customer site. In such situations, they may, quite naturally, be inclined to discuss an emerging issue among themselves. And quite probably, if they are problem solvers by nature, they are likely to reach a decision about how best to address it. With the very best of intentions, they may leave the employer out of the loop. And this, of course, is a problem.

Given these circumstances and people's very natural inclinations, it is particularly important for the vendor's manager to establish clear roles and guidelines with staff members. Among the requirements that ought to be on the list are regular attendance at the vendor's staff meetings and an established pattern of frequent phone calls or messages for the purpose of sharing current information.

There is another issue that managers and employees face in these off-site, matrixed-management situations. The customer's managers often have significant style differences from the vendor's managers. In addition, of course, the people filling those roles change periodically. All of this means that the vendor's manager has a special responsibility to help his or her employees work with their other supervisors. Sometimes this means taking on the role of a coach or mentor, or finding someone else who is particularly suited to do so. This can be a very time- and emotion-consuming process. Thus, a manager may find it difficult to carve out the time and energy needed when other pressing work—with milestones and measurable outcomes—sits on the edge of the desk. But in a service business, the people issues are critical to success, and so time must be found.

Reinforce the Company's Culture

Another issue unique to the outsourcing partnership is that of differing organizational values. Again, this arises particularly in situations where the training organization places an employee on site at a customer location. It is natural for this employee to become deeply enmeshed in the culture that surrounds him or her, and to begin to take on its values. Often this poses no real problem. But sometimes it raises very serious difficulties.

Example: Staying in Touch

CCFL employees who work in Corning's highly technical, highly intense Photonic Technologies Division become engrossed in the issues of that business—its growth, the transfer of knowledge to customers, the next wave of technology. That is as it should be. When they return to the training company that employs them for a staff meeting, however, they are in culture shock. CCFL may be talking about team issues, but they have not had contact with the Corning team in two weeks; so the team members who work at Corning begin to feel like they are in a foreign country.

The examples given here illustrate the kinds of problems that can arise. In the foregoing situation, the vendor was challenged to develop and use all appropriate means to ensure that its employees felt closer to it, without losing their closeness to the customers. The next example reveals the importance of having partnership managers who pay attention to the people and the day-to-day detail, as well as to the big picture. Clearly, the manager must have the skills to confront and resolve such individual personnel problems before they do serious, long-term damage to the relationship with the customer.

Example: Borrowed Behaviors

Another training firm had a small cadre of employees on site at a company that was undergoing a major overhaul of its information technology (IT) system. The employees were in daily contact with highly paid IT consultants who were jetting in and out of town. The nature of these consultants' work (and that of their entire organization) was to bring in powerful new systems, but to have no long-term responsibility for how well they worked. After a time, the training firm's employees became caught up in this mentality—and not a little envious that others were making so much more money than they were. For a training firm, where success is completely dependent on sustained, close relationships, with enormous attention paid to consistent quality and continuous improvement, these borrowed attitudes and behaviors presented a monumental problem.

One of the ways to preclude such problems—as much as they can be precluded—is to involve staff in regular meetings. It is helpful to hold two parallel streams of staff meetings: monthly meetings on operations and quarterly relationship-strategy meetings. The monthly operations meetings check milestones, measures, and deadlines to make sure the plan is on track. These meetings keep everybody informed about what is going on, not only in their own area, but in the whole training organization. This is the place to address the nitty-gritty of what is happening at various sites. It is also one way in which to ensure that all employees are connected with the larger organization.

The quarterly meetings reexamine the big picture. They review the relationship strategy with the customer, assess how well it is working, and try to anticipate changes that may affect it in the future. It is best not to mix operations issues into relationship meetings and vice versa. The rationale for this is that each deserves considered attention. Attending to details is likely to distract participants from bigger issues, and mixing larger issues into operations can allow people to avoid tracking measures that ensure real-world progress.

These means of communication flush out relationship issues, such as culture shock, and build in a mechanism for dealing with them. But there are still more communications concerns from a management point of view.

Refine Communication

Much has already been said about the need for communication, but here is a quick additional note for managers' consideration: Communication belongs high up on the list of priorities. It must be frequent. It must be consistent. And it involves not only telling, but listening. While these principles are no surprise, the organic changes implicit in an outsourcing relationship require that existing communication systems need to be rethought.

One of the tough things about communication is that it is sometimes hard to decipher and articulate what the partner needs to know. Those managers who intuit such things have a wonderful gift. Others must work hard at checking in, digging for understanding, and listening carefully. The onus is on both partnership managers. In order to partner well at this level, both need to probe for understanding of the other's needs, and be prepared to raise the germ of issues that they cannot yet clearly articulate.

Another situation that demands some rethinking and probable adjustment is the addition of new key players to an established team. It is easy for managers to continue talking with the same people they have always dealt with and then summarize the outcomes for the new person. It might also be easy to include the new person in every conversation, but that might not be the most appropriate decision either. In this situation, as in so many others, there are no hard-and-fast rules. The most useful guidance may come from revisiting the plan—in this case, the new person's role and responsibilities in the organization, and the individual performance goals—and thinking through such issues in that context.

Transfer Knowledge

One final issue for partnership managers to address is the transfer of knowledge. When training staff members are relatively isolated from the rest of their organization, they may not document their processes or commit their on-the-job wisdom to paper. When such a person leaves an organization, there is suddenly a knowledge gap. This can cause a serious interruption to service and allow real problems to creep in. Like many other issues, this one can be addressed by regular meetings with the vendor's manager or a coordinator who is assigned to oversee systems for a particular customer. In this way, decisions can be made about what needs to be documented on an ongoing basis, and reporting systems can be devised to ensure the transfer of essential knowledge.

CONCLUSION

This chapter is an assemblage of experiences in customer relationships, and the lessons learned from them. There is a lot of detail here—a lot to consider and remember. If it all seems overwhelming, it may help to focus on these three bits of advice:

- Use the planning process and tools at every conceivable stage. More than anything else, having goals, milestones, measures, deadlines, and assigned responsibilities will help managers and teams to understand where they are going and what they are going to have when they get there. It also will help to keep the process on track.

- Hire or assign the *right* person to the role of outsourcing manager. The role itself is critical to the success of this venture. No one would run a business without a manager. It would be very risky to operate this complex joint venture without one. And filling the job with a person with the unique set of skills and talents described above will pay back a hundredfold.

- Communicate widely, deeply, honestly, clearly, frequently, and consistently. It is the one thing that can be done to help allay fears, bring people on board, keep the partnership on course, preclude misunderstandings, and get the job done well.

References

Atlanta Consulting Group, Inc. (1991). "Partners in Quality: Build Strategic Alliances with Distributors and Other Suppliers to Increase Competitive Advantage and Provide Improved Service to Customers." Paper delivered at conference, Best Practices in Supplier Partnerships, Institute for International Research. 27–28 February, Orlando, FL.

Branning, John. (1997). "Developing Outsourcing Training Agreements." Paper delivered at conference, Outsourcing Training, International Quality and Productivity Center. 27–29 November, New Orleans, LA.

Bridges, William. (1991). *Managing Transitions: Making the Most of Change.* Reading, MA: Addison-Wesley.

Kepner, Charles H., and Benjamin B. Tregoe. (1981). *The New Rational Manager.* Princeton, NJ: Princeton Research Press.

Lacity, Mary, Leslie P. Willcocks, and David F. Freeny. (1996, Spring). "The Value of Selective IT Sourcing." *Sloan Management Review,* 13–25.

Venkatesan, Ravi. (1992, November-December). "Strategic Sourcing: To Make or Not to Make." *Harvard Business Review,* 98–107.

3

THE PROCESS OF
OUT-TASKING

3

OVERVIEW

As suggested in chapter 1, sometimes the need to source externally is limited to a well-defined, circumscribed activity. A company may need to offer a single, tailored course or discrete curriculum on a regular basis, but it does not have the right expertise internally. A training department intermittently may need help in designing or redesigning certain training programs. A change in computer systems may mean that a firm's registration process will be disrupted for an extended period of time, resulting in an immediate need for an external resource that will, in all likelihood, provide a long-term solution. All of these situations—and many more—are opportunities for out-tasking.

What differentiates these situations from outsourcing is size and scope. What distinguishes them from a standard customer-supplier relationship is the degree to which they partner. Although the extent of each project is limited to a single, clearly defined service or set of services, the partners get to know each other extremely well, work together in a seamless operation, and expect to maintain their relationship over the long term.

Example: Out-Tasking

For many years, CCFL has supplied Dresser Industries with customized training on several topics. The courses are delivered several times a year, always by the same instructor. This instructor maintains a relationship with Dresser's quality improvement team, and the courses are regularly reviewed, evaluated, and approved by the company's senior leadership team. In addition to providing instruction, the vendor markets the courses within Dresser and handles all registration via phone and e-mail. Between the outsourced sessions, Dresser's training in these areas virtually switches

---

(Example: Out-Tasking *continued*)

off. This relationship is an example of out-tasking in that it is clearly cir-cumscribed. Although the scope of the project is narrowly defined, the vendor partners with high-level managers to reshape the curriculum to meet Dresser's changing needs.

Another aspect of the out-tasking relationship is that it is frequently characterized by some urgency. The need often arises from sudden, unplanned-for changes. Retirements, resignations, downsizing, mergers, acquisitions, and other shifts in capacity often mean that a demand must be met quickly and well—and then maintained for the long term.

In such situations, the partners can make their analysis and planning process quicker and leaner than they might in a broader outsourcing partnership. There is one important caveat, however: What begins as out-tasking can often expand into larger relationships. Thus it is wise to build in checkpoints to review the partnership on a regular basis. At any time that it becomes apparent the relationship is expanding, the partners should invest in all the steps outlined in Chapter 2: The Process of Outsourcing.

THREE SUCCESS FACTORS

This chapter will provide information on the special issues and needs that pertain specifically to out-tasking. There are three factors that virtually always influence the success of an out-tasking arrangement:

- a compelling business reason to out-task
- a decision process
- well-defined roles and responsibilities

Compelling Reason

As is the case with total and selective outsourcing, there should be a compelling business reason for selecting the area to be out-tasked and the supplier to do the out-tasking. For example, a company's strategy might emphasize innovation as a way of developing new products or processes, or it might decide that developing a more diverse employee base would be critical to its success. One way to advance those strategies is through training. Perhaps the company's internal training department has expertise in these areas or the capability to develop such expertise. But quite possibly, an external supplier could bring more. Because the external firm has worked extensively with other companies on one of these issues, it may be able to tailor and deliver a better curriculum at lower cost than an internal education and training department could provide. With its broader perspective, such a firm can anticipate roadblocks and blind alleys, and thus save time, frustration, and money. In another example, some training firms now offer powerful, reliable registration and tracking systems. Using such an external resource may save a firm a considerable investment in hardware, software, and personnel in this functional area.

In either case, the decision to out-task projects such as these must be based on a compelling reason. And as with outsourcing larger projects, it is important to communicate this to all affected employees. Without developing and communicating the business case for out-tasking, managers doom the project to continual questioning, or even resentment and sabotage.

Decision Process

As with the more complex outsourcing explorations, the first job of the out-tasking decision team is to understand the very core of the company: its purpose, direction, key strategies, culture, and ways of getting work done. Although this analysis may not need to be as extensive as it would be in a proposed outsourcing situation, it is only with this kind of overview and perspective that a team can make wise decisions about which projects can best be out-tasked and which suppliers can best provide them.

At the heart of virtually every business decision is an assessment of the investment to be made. What is a project worth to a company? In training, particularly when considering sourcing options, the question of value is based on a continuum of learnings along a scale from "core" to "generic" (see figure 3.1).

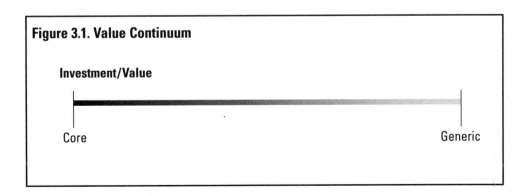

Figure 3.1. Value Continuum

Investment/Value

Core   Generic

The more the project is related to the core—a company's key directions, strategies, and goals—the greater the value. Conversely, the more generic the project, the lower the value. For example, leadership development programs are likely to have a high perceived value because a company's leaders exert so much influence over its success. This area is likely to be close to the core end of the continuum. On the other hand, presentation skills will fall toward the generic end. While improving employees' ability to make presentations means that meetings may be better focused and ideas more quickly understood, they are not the reason that a company succeeds or fails. Thus it could be expected that a training department would invest proportionately more time and money in leadership development than in presentation skills. Particularly when a company considers sourcing such areas externally, a clear understanding of the company's key directions and strategies becomes part of the cost-benefit analysis, and influences the size of the fee paid.

Not every situation is so clear cut, however. In the example mentioned above, innovation might be seen as core, or it might be generic. For a manufacturing company with aggressive growth goals, the development of new products and manufacturing processes is likely to be a critical part of its growth strategy. Businesses in computer, biomedical, and telecommunications industries are examples of firms likely to have such strategies. In such a situation, innovation training would likely have high value; it would be close to the core. For an organization whose success is far more dependent on successful marketing strategies or acquisitions, however, innovation training might have no value at all. Or its value might be limited to enriching the vocabulary of the sales group that dealt with high-tech customers, so they could better speak their customers' language.

Another tool useful in assessing training programs is a four-box matrix (see figure 3.2) that reveals which courses meet needs that are unique to the company and which are more generic, and also which areas are important to the company's strategic direction and which are important to its operations.

In most cases, companies are most likely to invest heavily in, and operate internally, those areas that are most unique to the company and most important to improving those areas it has defined as strategic. They are most likely to out-task or outsource those areas that are least unique to their organization and contribute to ongoing operation rather than to strategic initiatives.

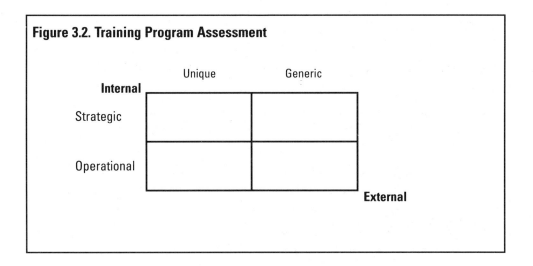

Figure 3.2. Training Program Assessment

	Unique	Generic
Internal Strategic		
Operational		

External

Roles and Responsibilities

Another factor that will certainly influence the success or failure of an out-tasking project is clear definition of roles and responsibilities for all players. Because people function on the basis of past expectations unless changes are made clear, it is imperative that the partners communicate clearly, honestly, and repeatedly with affected customers and staff. All employees touched by the out-tasking must clearly understand how the new relationship affects their work. Exactly what changes are made depend, of course, on the nature of the project. For example, if a course is being turned over to external trainers, it will be important to let the customers know what differences they can expect and to let the internal staff know what their roles and responsibilities will be with relation to the external team members. On the other hand, if the out-tasking involves completely changing the registration process from paper to electronic, this may require a significant marketing and training effort to let customers know how to access the site, what will happen when they do, and where to get help if they need it. Similarly, the internal and external staff will need to understand how to support this new direction and what outcomes they can expect: timing and accuracy of class lists, reports, cancellations, and other information they have either customarily received or that will be new to them.

> ### *Example: Clear Roles*
>
> *Faye Phillips, president of Phillips Training Systems, has long-standing out-tasking relationships with several clients. She believes strongly that clarifying requirements is the foundation for the success of such ventures. "If you have a trust relationship with your customer and you add value to what they originally ask of you, I think those are two of the main things that allow you to create the right environment for success," she says. "A lot of times our customers don't fully understand what their requirements are— or what their options are. So part of what creates the out-tasking relationship and enables success is our helping them to understand what might be involved. By doing a lot of asking and listening, we can really hone in on the requirements before we get started and do something wrong."*

While these success factors—compelling reason, decision process, and roles and responsibilities—cannot guarantee the success of an out-tasking project, they can certainly help to prevent its failure. Above all, however, following a process for making and implementing the out-tasking decision will have the biggest impact on the potential for the success of the project. The key steps in this process are described below.

KEY OUT-TASKING IMPLEMENTATION STEPS

While it is not always necessary to undergo as extensive a preparation and planning process for out-tasking as for outsourcing, there is still value in reviewing the outsourcing process steps outlined in chapter 2. In particular, out-tasking managers will benefit by paying particular attention to Steps 4, 5, and 6—Contract, Transition, and Manage and Improve.

Within this context, there are four implementation steps that are fundamental to the out-tasking relationship:

- Transfer knowledge.
- Define processes.
- Establish product and performance requirements.
- Provide for feedback.

Like those outlined in chapter 2, these are not necessarily sequential steps, but processes that may overlap. They will add value to virtually any proposed out-tasking project, regardless of whether it falls into the area of instruction delivery, course design, or any number of logistical areas.

Step 1. Transfer Knowledge

Once the decision is made to out-task a particular area, one of the first important tasks is to communicate a thorough understanding of the company to all representatives of the out-tasking partner that will interface with the company. There are two key questions to ask: What does the partner need to know? What are the best means or methods for providing that information?

In situations that are defined as out-tasking rather than more limited customer-supplier relationships, the goal of transferring knowledge is to enable the partner's representatives to behave as though they were the company's employees. While the fact of the out-tasking is not typically disguised, it is important that persons who are providing training or accepting registrations or answering questions about tuition reimbursement speak and act in such a way as to make the company's employees feel comfortable and confident. Thus the amount of company information shared is often greater than it might be in other vendor relationships. This communication of company knowledge should include four broad areas: business information, values and culture, initiatives, and policies.

The category of *business information* includes how the company makes its money: its range of products or services, the categories into which they fall, the broad markets in which they compete, or the customer groups they serve. Examples of this kind of information appear in chapters 4 through 8 in the introductory section titled "About [the organization]." In addition, of course, it is important to know the size of the organization. Is it a *Fortune* 250 company or a small firm with 100 employees and a budget measured in thousands rather than millions or billions? Who are its high-level leaders? Within such a broad context, the specific information that pertains to the project to be out-tasked will make infinitely more sense and have fewer opportunities to fail. Most companies publish materials that make this part of the knowledge transfer fairly easy. Annual reports, capabilities brochures, Web sites, or, for smaller organizations, product or service literature often provide a good base of information.

Values and culture are equally important parts of the company knowledge to be shared. Today many companies make written statements about their values. But many do not. In either case, it is still important to try to identify those principles that the company actually lives by as well as the ways that its employees interact. This is among the harder aspects to convey in the transfer of knowledge because companies, like other cultures, grow and mutate often without deliberate direction; they simply happen.

Much of this information is captured in a company's orientation program—videos, presentation materials, welcome packets, and so forth. Other layers may be evident in management training materials. These are likely to reflect how the company wants its managers to treat employees, if not how they are treated in actual practice. Company newsletters and intranet sites may also provide clues about the culture by reflecting what they choose to celebrate or recognize. Even with all of these materials, however, there is no substitute for visits and interviews that allow a prospective partner to ask questions and observe firsthand how people behave.

A company's *initiatives* are usually widely and frequently articulated, but this is not always the case. Initiatives are, in the language of total quality, the "vital few" toward which a company is driving. For example, under the leadership of now-retired CEO Jamie Houghton, virtually every Corning employee, customer, and supplier knew Corning's three major initiatives: quality, performance, and diversity. They appeared on posters, were talked about in every leadership presentation, were included in management objectives, and were the rationale for many specific programs. Essentially, these three initiatives communicated the cultural underpinnings that Houghton believed would enable the company to succeed. Again, such initiatives are likely to be found in documents like annual reports or their electronic equivalent. They may be even more explicitly revealed in internal documents. Often these are spoken rather than written, but transcriptions are usually available: copies of the CEO's major speech to the stockholders, key press releases, or the president's address to employees.

Finally, a company's *policies* are generally written and disseminated to managers or, in some cases, to all employees. The point here is not to know every policy governing every situation, but to have a good grasp of the major policies that guide life in the workplace—those on affirmative action or equal opportunity employment, the environment, health and safety, and other statements that guide behavior in important areas.

With all aspects of company knowledge, the goal should be to provide a broad general background to all of the out-tasking partner's affected employees, and then to enrich that with whatever specific information makes a difference to the project they are undertaking. There can be a great deal of variation in the latter, but the transfer of such information should always be guided by two key questions: What does the partner need to know in order to perform well in the situation? What will help the partner to develop an appropriate and comfortable level of understanding of both the content and the culture?

In large-scale out-tasking situations, this body of knowledge can be included in an orientation that the out-tasking partner provides to all those people who work on the company's project. The transfer of the company knowledge can be further expanded and reinforced by a number of practices, including pairing of trainers or other employees with parallel responsibilities and apprenticeships.

Example: Communicate Company Information

Corning Training Affiliates is a small group of independent consultants who work with Corning in a semipermanent relationship. Since they provide organizational development consulting and training in high-performance work systems in Corning's manufacturing plants, it is critical that they have not only a solid, broad understanding of the company's businesses, goals, values, culture, initiatives, and policies but also a very detailed and specific knowledge of the factories in which they work. At the beginning of the relationship, they were provided with an in-depth orientation and a body of relevant materials.

*Equally important, however, is for these consultants to be kept informed of changes as they occur. To this end, they are included in all relevant meetings, given opportunities to observe and ask questions, given extensive background training on the products and processes utilized in the factories where they work, and finally, undergo an apprenticeship. The latter pairs each consultant with a Corning employee with whom the consultant coteaches until they mutually agree that the consultant can handle the situation alone. This represents a big investment of time on Corning's part, but the stakes are high. They could not afford **not** to make such an investment.*

Step 2. Define Processes

Defined processes have proved their worth over time. They make it possible to have many different people perform the same activities in the same way, to identify and fix specific problem areas, and to standardize improvements. Thus they have particular merit in an out-tasking situation where the instincts and accumulated knowledge that may have guided long-term company employees are not available to external resources. Defined processes provide a means of quality assurance over the long term, and provide a real core of information that enables the partners to work together. Agreeing on critical processes helps to preclude disappointments and disagreements.

Early on in the out-tasking relationship, it will be important for the partners to document the processes that are currently in use, make any needed changes, and then agree that these processes will be used consistently over time. They also need to agree to review the processes regularly and understand that no changes to the processes will be made until both partners agree to them.

There are three important questions to ask with regard to processes in an externally sourced activity: Are they documented? Are they thorough? Are they followed? The first question has very specific implications. Processes should be mapped and committed to paper, where everyone involved can review them for gaps or errors, recommend changes, and ultimately agree upon them. Sometimes companies will have previously mapped processes that can be reviewed and discussed with their out-tasking partner. Often, however, these processes will need to be created. Some vendors develop processes for virtually every activity that pertains to a project. That often means creating one process for course design and development; another for reviewing off-the-shelf courses; another for instructor preparation or certification, another for tailoring courses from other vendors; others for various administrative processes—registration, payment, room setup, storage and delivery of materials; and finally, a process for changing the process.

In a situation where no process has been defined, the vendor should sit down with the partner and ask what it is that they want to have included. Because the vendor often has a base of experience with a number of partners, they are able to probe and ask questions that the customer may not have considered: How quickly and at what junctures do they need to know enrollment numbers? Does it matter to them whether the class discussions get noisy? Are there things they always want instructors to say?

After developing a first draft of a process map, the vendor sits down with the customer again and asks that they involve representatives of all the groups that might be affected. They walk through the process and ask the customer to identify areas where something could go wrong, or where there are missing steps. After all the refinements have been made, the vendor should ensure customer buy-in and also make sure to build in opportunities for review of the process as well as the products.

Armed with this assurance that the processes are defined and thorough, vendor managers are charged with ensuring that they are followed. In many cases, this means providing copies of them to people affected by the process and then developing additional tools that make it easy for them to understand their responsibilities, such as checklists and report forms that are submitted at various defined points in the process.

Step 3. Establish Product and Performance Requirements

Whenever a project is moved to, or started with, an external resource, it is imperative that the product specifications be clearly defined and that performance be equal to or better than the internal capability. One of the reasons for clarifying these areas is that there will be an automatic bias for "doing it ourselves," and mistrusting outsiders. In addition, there is a defined cost associated with using an external resource that cannot be disguised or buried in a larger budget. For both reasons, any project that is sourced externally is certain to come under scrutiny. Thus it will benefit both partners to establish clear performance standards and measures, to set these at least at the level of current company practice, and then to ensure that they are met. Anything less is very likely to result in disaster for the out-tasking partner and quite likely a "needs improvement" note in the internal manager's performance review.

Translating product specifications and performance standards into action means that a reviewer would be able to compare a set of specifications and standards to a course manual or an instructor's classroom management and identify whether they were being met. For example, product specifications for course design might require clear articulation of principles, the use of examples to illustrate each principle, questions for discussion, and a summary of key points. A reviewer would be able to determine very quickly whether each of these product specifications had been met. Performance standards are more difficult because in many cases they involve qualitative measures. For example, performance standards for instructors might include frequent eye contact with participants, engaging students in discussion in every class meeting, and periodically checking for understanding. While it is certainly possible to determine whether these things are being done, the quality of the interaction between instructor and students in each of these areas is harder to pin down.

Specific tools can be developed and used to ensure that an organization's defined product specifications and performance standards are communicated and met. Examples of such tools are course module checklists and tips for instructors. The first would help to ensure that instructors always complete a required list of actions related to teaching a particular course. The second helps to ensure a level of quality in teaching by providing helpful ideas and information to instructors. Examples of some of the materials that you can use to ensure performance standards are included in Appendix 1. The use of such tools helps prevent the hurt and disappointment that arise when there are hidden expectations. Even with the best efforts, however, surprises will occur. Since training is a human endeavor, it can benefit from the creativity and skill that people bring to it at every point along the path of course development and delivery. But this also means that it can suffer just as surely from differing interpretations, personal foibles, and the bad days that everyone experiences from time to time. For these situations, there is no remedy other than to try, try again.

Step 4. Provide for Feedback

Feedback provides a base of information that informs a continual improvement process as well as regular evaluations. This base of information helps to ensure that changes are made based on unbiased data rather than one or more individual opinions. Feedback processes should always be built into any out-tasking partnership.

The key questions to ask in planning for feedback are as follows:

- What do we need to know?
- How do we get information?
- How do we provide information to all the people who need to have it?

The question of what needs to be known usually begins with at least two different audiences. The first is the customer for the training product. In the case of course design and delivery, the customers are likely to be managers who pay for their employees' participation and are thereby entitled to certain expectations about the outcomes. Another likely customer is the training department manager who commissioned the project. In addition to the people who fill these roles, there is another layer of customers: the participants themselves. Each of these customers is likely to have expectations about the course, and they need to be built into the feedback processes.

For instance, a manager is likely to be concerned with how well the employee is able to translate the knowledge into application in the work setting over time. Given this expectation, the training firm might want to develop a tool that measures retained knowledge and the ability to transfer it to various applications at several checkpoints following the course. The participants' satisfaction with a course may involve this issue, but it is also likely to be based on the actual training experience: Did the instructor explain concepts clearly? Was there enough opportunity to practice learnings and get people feedback? Was the room comfortable? These expectations are typically built into a feedback form that is given to the participants at the end of each training session.

The partners need to agree on who the customers are, and then the external partner needs to clearly understand all of the customers' expectations. Based on this information, the out-tasking partner's staff can develop both feedback tools and processes. Again, it is important that the company's manager agree to these.

A number of tools can be used to acquire feedback. The following list suggests some of the major options:

- Observation
- End-of-course evaluation
- Customer reaction
- Database survey
- Performance appraisal
- Focus group
- Financial targets or comparisons

Each of these options has a number of permutations that can be developed to address the key question: What do we need to know? In addition to developing the tools and getting the partner to review and approve them, the supplier should write a process for administering them. This should include when it is administered, to whom, and by whom. It should also include a process for compiling and reporting the results.

The final issue in developing feedback processes is sharing the information. Certainly it will be important to provide relevant information to the various constituents. The instructor will best be able to meet or exceed standards by receiving regular feedback summaries from participant feedback forms, as well as from candid discussions following observations. The manager-customer will be more likely to fund the project if he or she has regular opportunities to review the knowledge-transfer measures and have input into course modifications. The training department customer will probably want to see a compilation of all the data.

APPLYING THE IMPLEMENTATION STEPS

If the managers for both out-tasking partners can stay focused on the four implementation steps and apply them to all of the areas where they might pertain, they will certainly move the project forward with some assurance of success. Table 3.1 provides a managerial tool for ensuring that these four steps are applied to various activities. As always, committing plans to paper may help managers to clarify and then follow through on them.

Using this tool implies not only that managers would identify what aspects of each step apply to the various tasks but also that they would follow through by creating action plans to ensure their implementation.

Table 3.1. Applying Key Out-Tasking Steps				
	Instruction	Design	Logistics	Other
Transfer knowledge				
Define processes				
Establish product and performance requirements				
Provide for feedback				

CONCLUSION

The four implementation steps outlined above by no means represent the complete wisdom about out-tasking. Each situation will be unique and will therefore hold its own exciting possibilities and alarming pitfalls. Chapter 2 may supply some additional guidance for prospective partners as they try to decipher their future and work through issues. In addition, a number of tips that can make the out-tasking relationship stronger and smoother appear in Appendix 2 in checklist form. They may serve as prompts, or reminders, for partners to be alert to additional issues and process steps.

Whatever the magnitude of the outsourcing or out-tasking project, both partners are best served by developing a very open and honest relationship, and by clarifying and committing to paper their mutual expectations for outcomes and the ways by which these will be achieved and measured. With this core of trust and solid quality practice, the odds of developing and maintaining a successful partnership are certainly improved.

4

COMPREHENSIVE OUTSOURCING: QUEST FOR A HIGH-QUALITY TRAINING SOLUTION

4

The Quest/CCFL Alliance example is included in this book for two reasons. First, it provides about as straightforward an example of comprehensive outsourcing of training as exists anywhere today. Like virtually all other successful outsourcing partnerships, this one has undergone some major shifts. It did not begin by fitting the comprehensive model, but it migrated there rather quickly. Second, this example reveals the development of an outsourcing partnership from the beginning of an organization. Like an increasing number of new companies, Quest was spun off from its parent company. The formation of this new entity provided a unique opportunity to build new systems from the ground up, and thus an excellent opportunity for growing a new outsourcing partnership along with the new company. In this way, too, the example may serve as a model for firms that arise from similar beginnings.

OVERVIEW

These days, the term *rapid change* has become a big, bold entry in the business lexicon. For a lot of reasons, Quest Diagnostics provides a glimpse of just how swift rapid change can be. It also provides a model for another increasing business phenomenon—a conglomerate in which a number of small companies are brought together through a series of mergers and acquisitions and ultimately become a single entity with a significant new presence. Like many other such companies, Quest has undergone a lightning-fast rebirth, complete with new leaders, new strategies, and new demands for

---

Incorporating interviews with Debra Turner, Quest Diagnostics, Inc.

training and education. Such companies have some unique—and often sizable—training needs as they work to create a unified organizational culture.

CCFL (College Center of the Finger Lakes) had provided services to Quest in an earlier incarnation, when it was Corning Clinical Laboratories, a wholly owned subsidiary of Corning Incorporated. Now the company is their partner in a comprehensive outsourced training and education service. They have worked together to understand the broader industry culture, Quest's multiple organizational cultures, and their training needs. Based on this information and Quest's new human resource strategies, CCFL developed a major portion of their curriculum and continues to implement these curricula, sometimes through its internal resources, but often as the manager of externally supplied services.

ABOUT QUEST DIAGNOSTICS

Today, Quest Diagnostics encompasses more than 16,000 employee-owners who process approximately 50 million requests from more than 75,000 physician-clients. In 17 regional laboratories, 14 smaller branch labs, and 200 rapid-turnaround STAT labs, Quest conducts testing and analysis of human fluids and tissues. They cover the gamut of laboratory testing, from the bedside to the highly esoteric. The bulk of their activity is routine—blood counts, Pap smears, pregnancy tests, cholesterol levels, AIDS-related tests, and substance abuse tests. In addition, the Nichols Institute operated by Quest is a leading provider of more complex esoteric immunoassay, cytogenetics, and molecular diagnostic testing for about one-third of the nation's hospitals.

Quest's origins were in a company called MetPath, Incorporated. Doctor Paul Brown founded MetPath in 1967 with a new concept for highly automated, high-quality, and low-cost testing. MetPath quickly grew to become the leading independent testing lab in the New York City area. Corning purchased MetPath in 1982, and, in the ensuing years, grew the business primarily through acquisitions. The company today reflects the 22 different companies that were assimilated into Corning Clinical Laboratories. In 1996, Corning spun off this medical testing business, and the company was renamed Quest Diagnostics (http://www.questdiagnostics.com, 5/14/98).

The name was chosen deliberately to signify the employees' dedication to the continuing pursuit of matchless quality in core testing and the relentless search for new knowledge and medical insights. They define themselves in terms of this vision: "Dedicated people improving the health of patients through unsurpassed diagnostic insights." The values to which they aspire support their vision: quality, integrity, innovation, accountability, collaboration, and leadership.

One key word here, however, is *aspire.* There is much to change. For not only does Quest still feel the impact of its 22-company origins, it also operates in a turbulent industry. This environment is characterized by tough competition, intense price pressure from government agencies and managed care companies, increasing deployment of technology, and a high employee turnover rate. In addition, of course, the entire medical industry is undergoing an unprecedented level of scrutiny by the government and the public, resulting in a perpetual aura of uncertainty. Added to these issues were some financial settlements predating Corning's acquisition of one of the companies and a sharp downturn in business during 1994 and 1995. Clearly, the new Quest faced some serious, even potentially life-threatening, business issues.

Thus, when Quest was formed as a new entity, company leaders proceeded to develop a powerful vision, mission, and values. In addition, they conducted as fast and as thorough an analysis of their own company and the entire industry as they could muster, and developed their strategies accordingly. They identified *skills development* as a critical success factor—a concept that was broadened in 1998 to *building employee capabilities.* They also recognized the importance of employee satisfaction, based on national research showing the correlation between meeting employee needs and increases in capability and competitiveness.

Four key strategies are now driving the people changes at Quest. The first is unification: Efforts are directed toward thinking, talking, and acting like one company. The other three human resources (HR) focus areas are: (1) develop and maintain a positive work environment; (2) retain and develop employees; and (3) be cost-effective. This, then, is the evolving environment and the broad direction in which the vendor serves as an outsourcing partner.

ABOUT CCFL

Founded in 1961, CCFL is a not-for-profit training and education organization that serves a nationwide client base from its Corning, New York, headquarters. Although the organization began as a consortium of colleges providing graduate and undergraduate degree programs, certifications, and continuing education units, it has evolved to become a leading supplier of training and development for business partners. The company provides comprehensive management of training and development programs, including course development and delivery and all aspects of their administration. In this role, it has developed courses in conjunction with business partners, evaluated external resources, tailored programs, and recommended and overseen the best fit with their partners' strategic needs. In addition, their immense database of resources, E&T Search, provides up-to-date information on a wide range of management and technical learning resources.

CCFL's relationship with Corning Incorporated has been recognized as a model for outsourcing-alliances-partnering by the International Society for Performance Improvement (ISPI), the American Society for Training & Development (ASTD), the American Productivity Center, and Linkage Incorporated. In addition, CCFL manages training and education for other large and medium-sized organizations and has been sought out by several *Fortune* 500 companies to consult on the establishment of outsourcing partnerships for training and education.

QUEST'S DECISION TO OUTSOURCE

Debra Turner, Quest's current learning and development leader, describes the decision to outsource in this way: "We made the decision to outsource in the fall of 1995 [Quest was still Corning Clinical Laboratories then], shortly after Kurt Fischer was named the new human resources leader. At that point, we had two internal trainers and one training manager. Since we were at a critical point in a volatile market, we needed to act with all deliberate speed. We knew we were lagging behind our competitors because of our lack of training. We could not afford the time to build our internal capability. So we decided to look at alternatives."

Fischer and his team reviewed three options: build internal capability, outsource, or ship employees off to external training. Two of the options were quickly eliminated. Given the key HR strategies, including the focus on reshaping the workforce into a cohesive single company, Quest needed to deliver training to all 16,000 employees. Building a staff with the capability to design, develop, and deliver the right training would take time—too much time, given the urgency company leaders felt to turn things around. At the opposite end of the continuum, sending 16,000 employees from multiple, and sometimes rather remote, sites around the country to training at external sites promised to be enormously expensive. Thus it appeared quite clear that outsourcing was far and away the best option to meet the company's needs for both the short and long term.

The decision to select their outsourcing partner was also swift. At the time, Corning Clinical Laboratories was still a subsidiary of Corning Incorporated, and had the opportunity to access much of Corning's infrastructure. "By all accounts, CCFL had been very successful in meeting Corning's training and education needs. They had expanded well beyond the original scope of services and proven their ability in a number of key areas," says Turner. "So we entered into negotiations early in 1996 and signed a contract in March."

BEGINNINGS OF THE PARTNERSHIP

Quest's partnership with CCFL began at a very different point from the original partnership with Corning. At the time that Corning chose to outsource, they had a well-developed curriculum and a well-established delivery capability. They were seeking to refocus their energies on strategic issues. Thus, they began outsourcing by handing off a limited number of courses for delivery only. Quest, on the other hand, was beginning much farther back in the process. Although in the early 1990s they had had a fairly sizable training department, that group had been dismantled when their business took a downward plunge. In addition, as noted, the business had undergone some dramatic changes. So Quest needed to start at the beginning: determining what they needed.

The new partners undertook a needs assessment at a broad level, categorizing their findings into five skills areas: leadership, management, supervision, functional, and individual. Quest then compared these findings with their strategic *Focus* document. At the first level of analysis, the fit was obvious. One of the critical success factors was skills development. The tougher question to answer was what to tackle first, given the business priorities. Based on information garnered from climate surveys, Quest decided that the highest and most immediate priority was to develop their supervisors' skills. This was the most direct route to improving employee satisfaction.

As Debra Turner notes: "The way we went about this was nearly opposite to Corning. Whereas Corning typically had developed their own curriculum and content with internal resources, we depended on CCFL to do the content work." The whole first year was spent performing very essential groundwork: doing the needs assessment, learning the industry and company culture, and developing the curriculum.

The supplier designed a short-term and a long-term solution. The first tier was a four-module program called Leading Your Team. This focused on delivering very basic skills and information on legal compliance issues: interviewing, sexual harassment, affirmative action, and equal opportunity employment. Quest put the whole organization (everyone with supervisory responsibilities) through this first course. The second tier was a supervisory skills certificate process, which Quest designed, with vendor participation on the committee. This curriculum was tailored very specifically to Quest's culture. Among other things, the fact that this program was designed as a certification process helped it to fit into Quest's culture. Because of the high need for accuracy and periodic changes in technology or protocols, the medical-testing industry has numerous certification and recertification requirements. Thus creating a supervisor effectiveness certificate process was an important long-term strategy.

Having addressed an area most likely to affect employee satisfaction, the alliance's second educational effort took aim at the other critical HR problem: high attrition. Late in 1996, they began to focus on educational programs for new employees. They redesigned their orientation program to address both employee satisfaction and compliance issues. "There are so many things an employee must know within a specified length of time," explains Turner. "For example, it's essential that they know what a blood-borne pathogen is and how to protect against it." The cross-functional team that designed the orientation curriculum included vendor representatives. Together, they designed a multifaceted program with a dual focus: compliance with legal requirements and formation of a uniform company culture. This module would be administered to all new employees within their first 60 days. It included the SMART (Self-learning; Motivation; Awareness; Responsibility; Technical Competence) process from Corning and the diversity module from the Bureau of National Affairs, Incorporated, along with pieces that were highly specific to Quest.

The partners have learned how to work better as a seamless organization. "From the beginning, we handed off a lot to CCFL," says Turner. "As soon as products were ready, CCFL actually came into our organization and trained our people in whatever had just been designed." The process of working together involves not only delivering what is already in the works but also refining the content and planning the next phases, a process that includes migrating to an open-enrollment system and redoing the needs assessment in order to scan the environment for what is changing.

CORE PROCESSES

As with any good outsourcing relationship, the Quest-CCFL arrangement is flexible. They have built a way of working together that enables them to identify and respond to changing needs. Table 4.1 reflects their current relationship and also includes some evolutionary changes, both past and anticipated.

As table 4.1 reveals, the partnership provides Quest with the comprehensive array of services they need. In terms of content, it spans the range from essential training administered to all 16,000 employees to highly specialized courses, consulting, or other learning opportunities to meet the specific needs of individual employees as they address developmental needs or prepare to take on new responsibilities. In addition, all of the functional areas are managed in a system that appears to all its customers to be Quest's internal training department, but is, in fact, largely staffed by the vendor.

There are a few areas that do not fit into this picture. One is sales training. Historically, the sales organization has taken responsibility for its own training. They have a whole curriculum, which is specific to their needs, and they contract directly with external vendors for some of its parts. In addition, a few of Quest's executives (the CEO and those who report directly to him) have worked directly with external vendors, most notably the Center for Creative Leadership. Again, this practice is based on relationships that predated CCFL's involvement.

One of Quest's early strategies was to identify the supplier's core competencies and hand off these entire functions wherever that was feasible. Thus, for example, there was never any question of how to handle the selection and hiring of trainers, the production and delivery of materials, or the identification of external resources. There was no value to Quest for them to invest resources in these areas. On the other hand, with their need to address some industry-specific regulatory needs and define their one-company unification issues, it made sense for Quest to take the lead in curriculum development on the first round of courses.

Table 4.1. Roles in Training Delivery

Functional Process	Quest Role	CCFL Role
Training and development needs assessment	• Identify strategic corporate needs • Determine priorities	• Assess direct customer needs; provide summaries and recommendations
Curriculum design and development	• Lead development of orientation and supervisory skills curricula; include CCFL on team	• Lead refinement of supervisory skills curricula and development of future courses; include Quest on team
Trainer selection and hire		• Screen Quest internal volunteer trainers • Conduct train-the-trainer sessions for internal instructors • Recruit and select external trainers • Contract with trainers
Trainer evaluation	• Shared with CCFL	• Shared with Quest
Production and delivery of training materials		• Manage process
Registration	• Was internal through 1997; may change as open enrollment begins	• Migrated to CCFL in 1998
Course evaluation	• Review results	• Manage process
Alternative learning resources (CD-ROM, distance learning)	• Exploring with CCFL	• CCFL exploring additional resources, developing additional capabilities
Scheduling and logistics		• Manage process
Identification of external resources	• Enable employees with unique developmental or training needs to access CCFL's E&T Search • Approval from supervisor required for registration	• CCFL's E&T Search is a database of more than 10,000 resources including a wide range of training, development, and consulting opportunities • Handle registration and negotiate fees

Quest continues to migrate more and more functional responsibility to the vendor. One of the keys to their success, however, is that they are managing the training and development process—and the outsourcing relationship—from a skilled and knowledgeable perspective. Quest has not given away their training function. Rather, they are very much in control of clarifying their needs and ensuring the desired outcomes. It happens that they are doing this with a tiny staff of their own; their extended staff is provided by the supplier.

LESSONS LEARNED

Over time, both partners have consciously and continually improved their ability to work together. They assess what has worked well and what could be improved at every milestone, and carry the learnings into the next phase of working together. They also stay alert for potential problems and take corrective action immediately. The lessons learned have been focused in the following areas: communication, use of new media, other external relationships, and resistance to change.

Communication

One of the things that had to be relearned was the critical importance of communication. The partners started with that understanding, planned an intensive schedule of "getting-to-know-you" activities, but then slipped a little as they all got caught up in the fast pace of production—the design and delivery of the first round of courses.

The first year, they invested heavily in getting to know one another. Quest invited the vendor to conferences, staff meetings, and site visits to individual business units. That investment of time up front has paid off handsomely. The second year, their communications lapsed a bit—they both recognized the need to improve and replan their communications processes. They now meet face-to-face in a monthly alliance meeting, part of which is devoted to Debra Turner giving an update of changes at Quest. In addition, the CCFL coordinator meets at least weekly with Debra in a scheduled telephone meeting. The inclusion of the vendor in Quest's voice-mail system facilitates rapid turnaround in discussion of ideas, updates on progress, and communication of decisions, even when both staffs are traveling or tied up in meetings.

E-mail has supplemented voice mail by adding the ability not only to converse via keyboard but also to send sizable training documents and slide presentations back and forth for review, editing, and updating. Both e-mail and voice mail are very forgiving of working across multiple time zones and work schedules that often involve unorthodox hours.

New Media

Quest has placed heavy initial emphasis on formal classroom training for two reasons. First, there was an urgent need to initiate some cultural change. The classroom provides a fairly effective and efficient way to do that, especially with large numbers of people. Thus the alliance's initial energies have focused on developing the first major blocks of courses and getting them up and running.

As Quest looks to the future and to the opportunities that are emerging through various technologies, it is asking excellent questions: How do we convey skills and knowledge without bringing people into a classroom? What cost-effective alternatives can we provide to the six employees working out of El Paso, for example, and other small clusters of employees in remote locations? What job aids can help to reinforce training that was taken three or six months ago? The advent of interactive software, multiple-link satellite transmission, video- and audiodiscs and tapes, and the Internet has provided an array of options that can be utilized to meet such needs. The challenge for the vendor now is how best to meet Quest's needs: invest in developing these capabilities themselves or manage one or several additional suppliers on behalf of Quest? Or does Quest develop separate relationships with other resources, with appropriate overlaps with the supplier as their work relates to courses it develops and administers?

Other External Relationships

Related to the latter is the broader issue of Quest's relationship with other external vendors. As Debra Turner has commented, "Because CCFL is not-for-profit, they can provide very cost-effective services. In addition to their own staff, they use many external vendors, and are often able to negotiate favorable rates because of the volume of business they bring to them. However, there are some commercial firms that do not give them a price break, and even a few who won't work through a third party at all." Thus the dilemma for Quest is whether to walk away from the services that some of these vendors are able to provide, or invest staff time and other resources in managing multiple partners. Quest is committed to maintaining the small size of its learning and development organization, and at some point, adding suppliers would unquestionably affect that.

Resistance

Any change yields a certain amount of resistance. Debra Turner reports that most of the resistance has been related to factors outside of the vendor. Some people have said, "Go faster," while others have said, "Too fast, too fast!" There has been some resistance to the cost of training in general, but Quest's HR department strongly believes that training is an investment that pays real dividends.

SUCCESS FACTORS

"When I think about the fact that we've only been doing this for two years, I'm extremely proud of where we are. It's staggering—in part because it sets the bar so high for the next two years!" These are Debra Turner's words, but they could just as easily come from anyone at CCFL's end of the alliance. The following factors have contributed to the success of the relationship—and to the successful outcomes for Quest: communication, total quality, and the seamless operation the partners have achieved.

Communication

Just as communication shows up in the lessons learned, it also shows up in the critical success factors. Despite seeing opportunities for improvement midstream, strong communication throughout has been an important contributor to the success of the alliance. In particular, both partners have worked hard at understanding the Quest culture and tracking the changes that are occurring, in part due to our mutual efforts in shaping the organization.

Total Quality

Because Quest spun off from Corning and CCFL has long been Corning's outsourcing partner, both organizations came to their relationship with a deeply embedded understanding of total quality—learned at one of the world's best practitioners of this discipline. So not only did they both know quality, they both knew the same version of quality. This has given them a large mutual vocabulary of standard practices: establishing goals with measurable outcomes; documenting, analyzing, and improving work processes and systems; making decisions based on data; recognizing and rewarding success; and most of all, an expectation of error-free work, the first time and every time.

Seamless Operation

CCFL has taken pains to create a system in which Quest's internal customers cannot tell that an external vendor is providing their training. Quest is not deceptive; they do not pretend that they have a large training department and no external supplier. But they treat the supplier as part of their organization, and in turn, the vendor's staff and instructors present themselves as part of Quest. There is a mutual effort on the part of both companies to understand and communicate their culture and to share what they learn with each other as well as with their own organizations. All in all, the Quest/CCFL Alliance can be seen as a successful example of a vendor serving a company that has undergone massive, rapid change.

References

Quest Diagnostics Incorporated. Answers to frequently asked media questions. Cited 14 May 1998. http://www.questdiagnostics.com.

5

ADMINISTRATIVE OUTSOURCING: A CLEAR EXAMPLE OF THE MODEL

5

This chapter provides an example of the most commonly used out-sourcing model: administrative outsourcing. The Dow Chemical–Delta College Corporate Services partnership is among the clearest examples of this model. Although the relationship has grown substantially and undergone some dramatic changes, its intent has remained consistent throughout: Delta is responsible for certain defined training logistics, leaving its partner free to focus on strategic initiatives.

OVERVIEW

In forming their partnership, Dow Chemical and Delta College Corporate Services (DCCS) discovered that they were on the doorstep of something very new for both of them. A work partnership began to emerge. But what did *partnership* mean? Dow had service agreements with other companies, so this part was not new. Delta had vendor relationships with other large companies, so they, too, knew the roles and responsibilities associated with the traditional contractual relationship. What each was looking for was a little different from the standard that both had already experienced. The vision was to have Delta employees on site in the Dow Midland Learning Center (MLC), working closely together and operating seamlessly to serve Dow employees in their development needs. Making this partnership a reality, however, was not a quick process.

Discussions between Dow human resources development (HRD) managers and the Delta executive director were the heart of the process. The way this partnership possibility was explored deviated from how Dow usually did things. The major difference was that no requests were sent out for other vendors to bid. Instead, the partner was chosen, *and then* the look of the agreement was explored and decided on. Since the whole idea of this sort of arrangement was new to both parties, they made a leap of faith and began the process. Questions about the feasibility of a partnership like this surfaced and were addressed. The Dow HRD manager and the Delta executive director worked together to benchmark other partnerships similar to their vision. They put together a straw man of what their partnership might look like and made adjustments as they went along. After they reached a tentative agreement, they then formed a transition team, in which they participated. The team, consisting of Dow and Delta employees, addressed all of the issues that would come up in the process of implementing this option. They took on such questions as the following:

- What would change for the employees currently in those positions?
- How would this affect the morale of the entire department?
- Specifically, how would the Midland employees react?
- What would happen to productivity in the short and long run?

The transition team made decisions using problem-solving tools, open discussion, and subteam approaches. They constructed a timeline and developed a purpose and desired outcome for each meeting. For example, a purpose would be: "Update team on status of the partnership, continue to resolve outstanding questions and issues, and plan next steps in the transition process of the partnership." A desired outcome might be: "Team will determine common understanding of where we are in the transition process and agree on what needs to happen next in order to continue moving forward."

The team researched legal issues for both sides, drafted service agreements, and looked at all of the other service organizations' agreements that would be affected, such as organizations that provide food, janitorial, and maintenance services for the training rooms. Then they planned how this partnership would be communicated, deciding to make the announcement simultaneously at both the Dow and Delta organizations. And they planned a celebration.

After seven months of formal transition-team dialogue and contract negotiation, a partnership was established in July 1993. The financial arrangement was set up to be a win-win situation for both parties. Although Dow's original intent was not to simply save money, Dow and Delta negotiated fees and working protocol in ways that were projected to show significant savings to

Dow, while at the same time provide Delta with a profit. The contract was a service agreement between Dow and Delta, but it was strongly set in the framework of a partnership.

ABOUT DOW CHEMICAL

The Dow Chemical Company, founded in the 1890s, is the fifth largest chemical company in the world, with annual sales of more than $20 billion. Dow manufactures chemicals, plastics, energy, agricultural products, and consumer goods, which it supplies—along with environmental services—to customers in 157 countries around the world. Headquartered in Midland, Michigan, the company operates 115 manufacturing sites in 37 countries and employs approximately 40,300 people worldwide.

In 1992, as part of their strategic planning, the leaders of Dow Chemical looked at key issues that would influence how the company would do business in the future. Like so many other U.S. companies, Dow was feeling the effects of global competition and shrinking dollar resources. The corporate leaders knew that changes had to be made. They had many difficult and thoughtful decisions ahead of them—decisions that would center on Dow's core business, its expertise, and the areas that could yield the greatest potential growth. In making those decisions, leaders took a hard look at those areas that were not Dow's core business. They began to analyze whether the needs they met might be better served by partnering with other organizations whose core businesses matched them. One service area Dow scrutinized was the delivery of employee development programs. In 1993, following this analysis, things started to change.

Historically, the culture of the company has been basically traditional. A patriarchal system was in place, and employees' development was the responsibility of the supervisors. Employee reviews included training suggestions or mandates. Growth and movement in the company was a direct result of the supervisor-employee relationship and review process. Climbing the ladder through many levels of management or incremental specialist steps was the path most employees traveled to be elevated. One thing that moved them toward higher levels was a required number of training hours to be completed each year.

The Employee Development (ED) Group was one of the resources for the employees to get this training. They decided which courses would be offered, performed companywide needs assessments, and implemented, for the most part, classroom training. All activity related to classroom training was the responsibility of the ED Group. The Midland-centered ED employees' work generally centered on the corporate headquarters, with some reach into other parts of North America.

There also were ED employees at the major sites around the globe. They all were assessed on a body count, that is, their ability to fill the chairs in classrooms. ED was not the only training group in Dow, however. Groups within various businesses and departments provided training for their own units. For instance, the Plant Operations Group had employees who developed and delivered training for the specific needs of the plant. The Marketing and Sales Groups provided some training specifically geared to those areas as well.

The role of the ED Group is reflected in the list of training programs they offered, which fell into the following four broad areas:

- Interpersonal Relations—listening skills, social style, telephone skills, and other communication skills.
- Personal Effectiveness—writing skills, time management, and presentation skills.
- Supervisory and Team Building—meeting management skills, coaching, facilitating team projects, and management tools.
- Personal Growth—courses that looked at current positions and helped employees fill skills gap requirements.

In many cases, these courses looked different in different parts of the world. The philosophy was global in focus. Information was shared, but it was not a priority for all of the training courses to have global standards. The cost and feasibility of that kind of effort outweighed the desire for standardization.

As in other parts of the company, a new focus emerged for the ED Group in 1983. Its new role became performance improvement consulting—defined as consulting with the customer and looking for whatever intervention would be most effective, rather than just offering a traditional training class. It required ED staff to get out into the organization, become more visible to employees, and meet their needs where they worked, rather than have employees come to them. All of this meant that less time could be spent on training-implementation activities, such as registration, materials management, room setup, and the like.

At this point, it was decided that the ED Group was not in the business of performing these training-administration activities and that their efforts should be focused on consulting. So they had to ask whether they should still offer classroom training. Looking closely at what Dow leaders now wanted the employee development area to provide, the ED staff agreed that individual and team skills building was still important. They also decided that some classroom training would be offered as an option for performance improvement, but at the same time they began to explore other options in the consulting process. Like others in internal organizations, the ED staff recognized that the company as a whole was downsizing and eliminating jobs. This factor, among others, influenced them to choose a new strategy: to outsource their training administration and delivery needs, specifically those implemented at their corporate headquarters site in Midland, Michigan.

ABOUT DELTA

Delta College Corporate Services, a semiprivate, self-supporting company dedicated to providing workforce training, was created in 1983 by Delta College, a public community college. Today Delta broadly defines its mission as "helping customers achieve success through people and technology." The organization "provides training, consulting, development, and management services for workforce development. Delta's firm commitment to educate local businesses led to [its] presence in the national and international marketplace, serving over 800 companies in 43 states and 53 countries" (http://maps.-nemonline.org/maps/MRS385.asp, 8/8/98).

When Dow began to consider outsourcing, they discovered that Delta had experience working with other businesses and had established a positive reputation in the community. For some time, Delta had provided customized training and delivery to numerous markets such as automotive, skilled trades, quality center, computers, and public service. In fact, Delta already had contracts with some other organizations within Dow Chemical.

HOW THE PARTNERSHIP DEVELOPED AND GREW

As part of the transition and ongoing discussions, some decisions about roles and responsibilities were made. Dow would continue to determine what training interventions would be offered. They also retained responsibility for the strategic direction that training would take. Delta was given responsibility for administrative functions. This outsourcing of administrative functions would allow Dow ED employees the time they needed to help the businesses find effective performance improvement solutions—their new organizational mission. Thus Delta gained responsibility for managing training classes and meetings for the MLC at Dow corporate headquarters. These responsibilities included the following:

- scheduling classroom space
- configuring each classroom to meet individual needs
- scheduling meeting space with the same attention to configuration needs
- managing the registration process, including confirmation of enrollment, and monitoring participation for cancellations
- conducting facilitator evaluation and management of data
- acquiring and managing training materials
- managing contracts with the food service, maintenance, and other contract-service providers to the learning center

The new configuration of responsibilities is reflected in the positions designated for each partner, as shown in table 5.1.

The partnership began with a spirit and commitment to make the arrangement succeed for the benefit of Dow employees. From the beginning, one strategy for achieving this success was to make the partnership seamless and transparent to the Dow population. Delta would reside at Dow's learning center site, and its presence would not be readily apparent to the employees using

Table 5.1. Employee Positions at the Midland Learning Center	
DOW CHEMICAL **Midland Site HRD**	**DELTA COLLEGE CORPORATE SERVICES** **On-site Midland DCCS**
5 course managers 5 office professionals/training assistance 1 instructional designer Dow facilitators • 2 setup • 1 office professional/facilitator scheduling • DCCS facilitators	MLC manager 2 registration associates 1 MLC scheduling 1 materials 1 reception/focal point

the center. This decision was made in order to help Dow employees with the transition and to minimize the concerns that surround this type of change. With the downsizing Dow employees had already experienced, new faces and names in the training function had the potential to cause feelings of distrust and lack of loyalty toward Dow.

The partnership faced one very real struggle: the anger and resistance of Dow employees whose responsibilities were being taken over by their new partner's staff. Employees also were asking questions: Is this necessary? What's wrong with the way we did it before? What will we lose? How will we control quality? Will we lose our culture? At the same time, Delta employees' needs also had to be recognized. The benefit to them of keeping the partnership seamless was that it made it possible for them to concentrate on doing the job rather than on defending the partnership.

Over the first few months, the real working relationship developed. Dow and Delta became "we," as team members worked together to reconfigure the tasks and improve the operation. Together, they scrutinized many processes and created more effective and efficient ones. When the partnership began, the administrative training functions were divided by job, which worked well in the sense that each function had subject matter experts. Each of these employees concentrated on one aspect of the implementation process and could spend time and energy on making their particular cog in the machine work well. The team decided that this structure would be maintained. The challenge it presented was that people found it difficult to understand how the other cogs operated, and how their part affected the whole.

The first step in addressing this problem was to look at the communication processes. The team analyzed how the decision makers for the course content communicated with the implementers, applying two questions to each course: Why are we doing this? and What is this information used for? Tasks and processes were changed or eliminated if they were not deemed value-added. Then, people in each function asked not only the decision makers but also one another, What do you need from us? Based on the information these discussions generated, new, more usable reports were developed on training activities. These answered such fundamental questions as who attends a course, how many participants are canceling, and when, what are the charges for each session.

By sharing information, understanding others' needs, and working together to form new processes for a common understanding, the team was better able to examine issues, predict bottlenecks, and develop solutions. One solution proposed was a new communication tool: the Change Request form. This two-sided form was the core document that triggered an orderly and complete change process. For example, if a new class was added to the system or if the maximum number of participants allowed in a class was changed, this request form was used. The person making the change initiated the form, and each function received the necessary information, made the change, and initialed it before passing it on to the next function. This process has been improved as needed and is still an effective tool. It has made a significant difference in reducing errors and oversights.

Taking Stock at 18 Months

About 18 months into the partnership, an objective joint review documented many changes. As the Dow ED Group began to shrink, more work shifted to the Delta side of the partnership. Delta took on additional responsibilities in facilitator coaching, facilitator communication, and education activities. One full-time person was added to the Delta staff to respond to this need. Another major change was the addition of course management responsibilities to the Delta team. This included working closely with the Dow sponsors on revisions and feedback; working directly with participants who had questions about the content of courses; keeping facilitators aware of content and content changes; setting up special sessions; coordinating with the instructional specialist to set up and run train-the-trainer classes; tracking the evaluations and responding as needed; keeping abreast of current trends; and exploring and sharing alternative training course methods with Dow partners. Furthermore, Delta took over the upkeep of the classrooms and equipment in the MLC. The interface and oversight of the janitorial and food services became a Delta responsibility. The learning center manager chaired a facilities team that was composed of all parties, and had responsibility for the smooth operations of the center. Delta also assumed responsibility for the Midland Learning Center Resource Library—organizing, cataloging, inventorying, and creating a database for the borrow-and-return system. In addition, the marketing of the course offerings that Dow provided to its employees was transitioned to Delta.

Some of these responsibilities included a host of new tasks. For example, in response to the facilities responsibility, Delta created a new learning center inventory method. Other large Dow groups were beginning to utilize the learning center for needs other than training, and Delta staff members found themselves hosting, organizing, conducting, and generally overseeing very large special projects that arose.

In response to Dow's growing needs, Delta added more registration and course coordinator positions. It also restructured and added additional part-time help to come in on an as-needed basis. Dow's own analysis showed that they were enjoying significant cost savings in general overhead and course-facilitator expense, without suffering a loss of quality of delivery.

PARTNERSHIP EVOLUTION THROUGH 1996

Like any blending of two organizations, the Dow-DCCS partnership has been strongly affected by the changes within each partner organization. Dow's push toward globalization and the significant changes in its approach to HRD drove major changes at Delta—and in the partnership. The result has been a certain amount of upheaval. But out of that has come an incredibly fast learning curve and growth in all aspects of the partnership.

Dow Chemical: Reengineering for a New Global Perspective

A number of transitions have occurred within the Dow ED Group. First came a change in name from "employee development" to "human resource development," and an increasing focus on the company's global operation. As business needs drove the company culture to change, it became apparent that the HRD processes also needed to change. A new global perspective for human resources (HR) led to a reengineering of the entire HR function, which began in the early months of 1996. The Dow HRD director created four leadership teams to strategically benchmark Dow practices:

- Consulting Services Team—to benchmark the intellectual property of Dow for outsourcing.

- Employee Development Team—to benchmark the employee development process and position function responsibilities.

- Learning Action Team—to benchmark all current training practices within Dow Chemical globally (a daunting task previously not attempted).

- Change Management Team—to benchmark the change process needed to move Dow employees from a patriarchal corporation to a flatter, employee-empowered corporation.

These four Dow Chemical action teams were charged with researching and recommending a new HRD structure. In September 1996, they presented their suggestions for redesign, which Dow adopted. This new structure was designed to promote the global perspective they were looking for. It consists of four major categories: Global Process Leaders, Learning Systems, Organization Effectiveness, and Resource Center Implementation Leaders. Smaller categories also exist including Employee and Career Counseling, Global HR Systems, Communications Technologies, and HR Global Suppliers Services. The relationship among these areas is illustrated in the organization chart in figure 5.1.

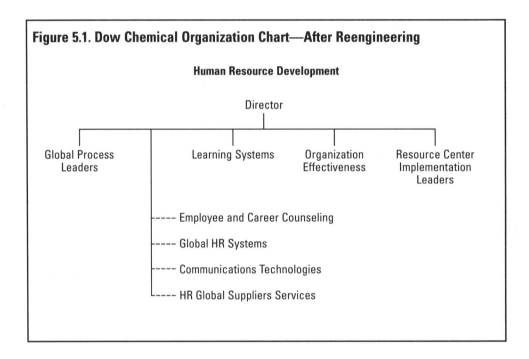

Figure 5.1. Dow Chemical Organization Chart—After Reengineering

Human Resource Development

Director

Global Process Leaders | Learning Systems | Organization Effectiveness | Resource Center Implementation Leaders

----- Employee and Career Counseling

----- Global HR Systems

----- Communications Technologies

----- HR Global Suppliers Services

The global process leaders are responsible for one or more of the global competencies identified for Dow employees to master. Their responsibilities include providing interventions that enable all employees to fulfill these expectations. One of the first tasks for these leaders has been to review all of the training Dow Chemical offers globally and to determine the standard offering for the entire organization.

The context for the global process leaders' efforts is the new approach required by the flattening of the organization. As the jobs that people once aspired to began disappearing, career paths for Dow employees became unclear. Employees needed to know how to grow in the new organization. A new employee development process was created, in which employees now take responsibility for developing their own skills and expertise, as well as for identifying future roles. While employees have responsibility for managing personal development, their supervisors are responsible for providing the support and counsel necessary to this process. Tools are provided, such as a 360-degree feedback tool and a navigator tool, to help employees find an intervention to address identified needs.

In order to have a measuring stick against which to compare individual skills and knowledge, global process leaders have responsibility for the creation of competency profiles for various categories of work. These competencies are clear definitions of the company's expectations for each role within job families. Competencies are a combination of knowledge, skills, and behaviors that have been identified as critical to Dow's and the employees' success. These include global competencies, which apply to everyone at Dow regardless of function or role, as well as functional competencies, which define technical competencies. Thus the work being done by the global process leaders is critical to Dow's new competency-based people development approach.

The other three major categories are easier to describe. The learning systems group is the development team. If an intervention needs to be developed or an activity needs to be redesigned, this group takes on that responsibility. One example of such a redesign effort is to re-create an activity as an intervention to support a competency. The organization effectiveness team acts as a consultant group in reengineering and other process-oriented consulting. Leaders of resource center implementation, the function with which the Dow-DCCS partnership is aligned, carry out the training programs themselves.

Delta College: Restructuring and Growth

With Dow's restructuring came restructuring for Delta. The way the partners had worked together up to this point had to change. Delta's responsibility for course management and instructional services was transitioned back to Dow and absorbed into the new HRD structure. Researching new training or professional development opportunities was assigned to the global process leaders. The instructional services area was reassigned to the resource centers. These new groups within Dow are learning how to work together and developing new systems of communication and work processes. One of the challenges is to create infallible methods for passing information within groups, as well as to other groups who must work with them. While many gray areas still exist, time is being dedicated to defining clear areas of responsibility.

Another area that underwent change was that of facilitation and Dow employees' participation in it. Facilitation is offered as an opportunity for growth and personal development. As a result of the general downsizing and reengineering, however, Dow employees who previously facilitated HRD courses have become focused on their own steadily mounting core responsibilities. Fewer Dow employees are responsible for more outputs, leaving little time for facilitating. In light of this, fewer and fewer Dow employees are available to fulfill this important role. As a result, Delta is beginning to supply more contract facilitators to meet this need. Previously, Delta had provided facilitator support for a limited number of courses, generally at the Midland site, and only occasionally at other locations. Now Delta is expanding its facilitator base and sending facilitators to other North American sites. This involves more travel time, reducing the classroom training hours that Delta can provide. Another challenge Delta faces is finding a larger pool of professionals who are able to come up to speed quickly on the content of courses, and who already possess facilitation skills. To meet these needs, more train-the-trainer programs have to be run, requiring huge time commitments from Delta, as well as more dollars from Dow.

There are other changes for Delta College Corporate Services. One change is that it has taken on new responsibility for the administration and coordination needs of other training groups within Dow. For example, it now administers the non-HRD-sponsored training done by groups within the information systems and computer training functions. These new responsibilities include coordinating with many Dow sites that they had not previously worked with, expanding Delta's reach beyond the North American region to Europe and Latin America. Delta also began to provide full training administration services out of the MLC site. To staff these growing responsibilities, Delta created two full-time positions as liaisons and coordinators for these groups. Session numbers processed for these groups have now surpassed those processed for HRD. This expansion was not explicitly planned for; it evolved.

As Delta provided successful local training administration and the needs for functional training increased, its responsibilities increased. For example, one of the functional groups decided to consolidate training administration for at least two major regions to Midland and Delta. Generally, the concentration of sessions offered is in North America and Europe. This means that Delta collects information on needs; creates schedules based on those needs; and processes rooms, facilitators, and materials all through Delta in Midland. They also provide follow-up to the training by gathering the rosters, assigning credit for the courses, and processing any accounting needs.

Again, this expansion evolved very quickly. Delta found that advance planning for this kind of growth was next to impossible in Dow's rapidly changing environment. One key strategy that worked well in accommodating this major new demand for service was flexibility in staffing and other resources. Cross-training made it possible to move existing employees into more complex areas, and to benefit quickly from the addition of new employees by initially giving them simpler tasks. This reduced transition time and helped to ensure the continuity and smoothness of operations. And as with all other aspects of the organization, the partners again benefited by insisting on good communication and using the communication tools and processes that had been developed with previous projects.

December 1996 marked the beginning of an intense and fast-moving undertaking for HRD. The focus was a major new Dow management training effort. The scope was again global. Delta implemented training that took place simultaneously at five different locations around the world, with a range of one to three sessions per day at each site. Sixty-six sessions took place in a six-week period. Delta registered 3,000 participants; coordinated and shipped materials; scheduled and tracked two leaders and five coaches for each session; and developed and maintained lists and charts for accurate, up-to-date information made accessible via file servers to employees who needed it throughout the world. In addition, Delta provided all the recordkeeping associated with implementing this training.

Clearly, this project demanded that the partners rethink how they operated. They used technology for communication and registration in a way that had not been done before. Dedicated e-mail lines were put into place, and file servers were set up. The Dow-DCCS alliance was catapulted into the global focus Dow was seeking.

WHAT HAS WORKED WELL

During the process of developing a partnership, Dow and Delta have focused on a number of successful strategies.

Teams

The most effective and important strategy used to make this partnership successful has been the team approach. The word team refers to people working together toward a common vision, negotiating, helping one another solve problems, pitching in when a function becomes overwhelmed, and counting on that help coming back when the situation is reversed. It means keeping others involved and informed. As a team, the partners take full advantage of the synergy created when they work together, giving special attention to the following issues: communication, multiple perspectives, process improvement, and flexibility.

Communication

Good communication—and lots of it—has been essential. The vehicles used regularly include e-mail, meetings as appropriate, one-on-one discussions, and audio- and videoconferencing. The fundamental principle underlying the communication effort is to let everyone on both sides of the partnership have sufficient information that they feel—and are—a part of all decisions. Whether this takes the form of direct responsibility for making decisions or providing input to help guide them, everyone has both an opportunity and a responsibility to contribute. Good communication also has been critical in enabling the partners to manage constant change and lessen the potential jarring impact such change can have on work and relationships. Another advantage of good communication is the absence of redoing processes or getting blindsided later because the team missed an important step along the way. Getting all the appropriate players involved has saved time and money.

Multiple Perspectives

Another area of attention has been diversity of work styles and work groups. The partners want not only the key stakeholders but also the players with different perspectives to have input on important decisions. The details as well as the big picture have to be represented, so that a project can be examined from as many different points of view as possible. If this is not reasonable, the team looks at what is missing in terms of focus and processing information and makes an effort to spend time in those areas.

Process Improvement

A third area that significantly affects success is a willingness and determination to undertake process improvement. The partners have worked hard to get rid of "sacred cows" and to take a fresh, honest, and tough look at their processes. As they do this, they decide what adds value and what needs to be improved. Each new project provides the opportunity to take another look. As part of the process improvement effort, Dow and Delta continue to streamline and make full use of technology whenever possible.

One major example of a long-standing, complex process that underwent significant improvement was registration. The old system utilized forms filled out by hand, with recordkeeping on a flip-file rack. In anticipation of increased demands for more types of information to be delivered in a timely manner, the partners realized that the paper system would present difficulties. They brainstormed and analyzed new ways of completing the registration process tasks, ultimately deciding to create an electronic system that would not only make the system faster but also broaden the scope of what they could do with the information entered. Dow bought this system, a database software package, but both partners were involved in custom designing it to meet their needs. Some of the challenges they faced were resistance and concerns about technology. One of those very real concerns was that if this system went down, they would be virtually paralyzed; so they included a back-up process for those situations. Then, in minute detail, they developed the electronic system. This task took a long time, and it was difficult to maintain a paper system while trying to convert to an electronic one and still meet customer-service objectives. The partners successfully completed the system prototype and soon moved to the more permanent system, resulting in a far more efficient process.

Flexibility

Flexibility in a constantly changing environment also has proved to be a valuable strategy, but not one that was easily accomplished. Dow and Delta have learned to really pull together when large projects come along. Their ability to handle such projects comes largely from cross-training. They have built in shadowing time and cross-functional flows, and have required each function to get input from—or have discussions with—others, to ensure that changes are not going to adversely affect another area. Cross-training not only helps get the work done by enabling team members to step in and help the function with the biggest workload, it also provides everyone with an understanding of other functions and their needs. This has enabled everyone to see the bigger picture, which has proved enormously helpful in decision making.

Another key to being flexible is staffing. The Delta partnership team has maintained a mix of part-time and full-time personnel. As needs change, the schedules of part-time employees can be expanded or contracted to meet the demand. Similarly, full-time employees are able to flex their work schedules to meet customer needs. For instance, if there is a very heavy workload in the materials-management area, employees can extend a workday or two to handle the project needs, and lighten their hours later in the week. They also employ student workers who can come in on an as-needed basis.

THE DIFFICULT AREAS

With 20/20 hindsight, Dow and Delta now realize there are some things they would try to do differently or better, if they had the opportunity to do them over. Some problems may not yield to different approaches; they will always be difficult. But for those who are considering the formation of a partnership, the following areas of concern may be worth considering at the outset: contracting, employee anxiety, and the legalities of employment.

Contracting

One of the lessons learned was that underdefined areas of responsibility in the contract can cause confusion and anxiety as partners move into the new relationship. Quite deliberately, the Dow-DCCS partnership initially left some areas in their contract gray. The contract was negotiated to cover broad categories of work, with the actual details to be worked out as the work came up. The real benefit of this arrangement was that it helped to develop the mindset of a partnership rather than a traditional contractual arrangement.

The very general nature of the contract, however, sometimes made it quite difficult to determine whether work was fairly compensated. For example, the broad contractual category Monthly Fees covered all fees except for facilitation, course materials, course catalog, training supplies, equipment, and maintenance. The facilitator costs were negotiated on a services-rendered basis. As other Dow customers looked to Delta to provide services, it became difficult to predict what the fees should be. In some cases, the workload turned out to be much greater than anticipated, and there was no avenue to recoup the cost. It was difficult to know how to staff for projects, due to the general nature of the contract, or how many hours would be required. In some cases, this was merely a result of lack of experience with similar projects. The partnership could not use the contract as a tool to judge time and effort in order to allow fair compensation and staff coverage.

In the fourth year of the partnership, Dow and Delta knew that the way fees were paid had to be changed, because future expansion and good customer service were going to be hampered under the existing contract structure. A great advantage to both Delta and Dow was the willingness of Dow's management and purchasing department to view the contract as a living document. This allowed them to refashion the contract on a continuing basis. A major effort was made to clarify roles and responsibilities. Fees were based on scheduled training sessions, with separate categories for facilities management and special projects.

Employee Anxiety

Another difficult area was employee anxiety about job security, ownership, and quality. This occurred on both sides of the partnership. Giving up responsibilities was hard for the Dow employees who had maintained many of the job tasks that were transitioned to Delta. With all the changes Dow employees were experiencing, they were asking themselves, Will I have a job? and If they are not Dow employees, will they care about the quality as much as we do? Will they have Dow's best interest at heart? The Delta employees experienced similar anxiety about taking on new responsibilities and about their ability to learn fast enough and absorb all there was to learn. They too were asking themselves questions: Will I be able to do and keep this job, or will I have to do this job twice as well as a Dow employee to be considered a quality worker? Will I be able to understand all of the Dow issues I need to? Will I fit into Dow's culture? The partners dealt with team members' anxiety by bringing these issues out into the open and discussing them. Team meetings were helpful. In addition, they were able to alleviate some of the stress through task forces on trust, empowering employees, establishing clear measures for success, and emphasizing communication.

Legalities of Employment

Legalities surrounding employment issues presented another area that required special attention from each partner. Dow had to be careful about where and when Delta staff members were treated as Dow employees. Living on site presents special problems in that regard. Every activity, team meeting, and shared function could potentially cause a co-employment problem in the legal sense. The partners have learned to cooperate as a team and work with the legal issues. Co-employment mistakes could certainly have been costly to both parties.

CONCLUSION

In summary, new challenges have continued to arise as the partnership has moved forward and grown. Fortunately, Dow and Delta have built a strong foundation from which to grow. They are able to confront each new challenge head on, openly discuss it, and problem solve until an equitable solution is found. As more new challenges come along, the processes, the relationships, and a can-do attitude will move them forward. The partners are confident that they will continue to face future challenges and arrive at the same kinds of positive outcomes they have experienced in the past. All of this will be possible because of fundamental ways of working together: learning from mistakes, always remembering the people, and *together* continuing to succeed.

References

Michigan State University Board of Trustees. Delta College Corporate Services. Cited 8 August 1998. http://maps.nemonline.org/maps/MRS385.asp.

About the Contributor

Pam Burgess manages the expanding training partnership between Delta College Corporate Services and the Dow Chemical Company HRD Resource Center in Midland, Michigan. Her responsibilities include managing the Midland Learning Center activities and staff, as well as acting as a focal point for all training and consulting activities that occur between Delta and Dow. In addition, she facilitates numerous courses, meetings, and consulting interventions for all levels of the organization.

Pam is certified as a trainer for many national vendors, including programs for Zenger Miller, Wilson Learning, Blanchard Training, Franklin Covey, and Myers Briggs. Her experience in the field of performance technology has included not only facilitation but also design and implementation of program changes and upgrades; coordination and customization of special sessions; development and monitoring of evaluation instruments; and recommendations for cost reductions.

6

THEMATIC OUTSOURCING: ALIGNING TRAINING WITH STRATEGIES

6

Compaq's experience is included in this book for three reasons. First, it provides a look at thematic outsourcing, a model that is often considered by those who explore outsourcing. In this model, a partner is sought based on certain themes, or expertise, in broad subject areas. Although Compaq changed course from this original direction, its initial process does reveal how the company went about the search for a partner in a theme-based outsourcing model. The second reason that Compaq's experience bears examination is that it did, in fact, shift to a different model—one that more closely resembles the logistical outsourcing experiences seen in the partnerships of Corning and Dow Chemical. What is particularly interesting about this is that, to date, most other firms that started their outsourcing journey with the intent to use the thematic model have wound up changing course. Finally, this example is included because it reveals both how difficult the early part of the journey was, and how perseverance and the resolve to make radical changes have paid off.

OVERVIEW

In the space of three years, Compaq's corporate human resources (HR) organization worked sequentially with three different outsourcing partners. What began as a search for a partner with special expertise in leadership development soon became a search for a partner that could provide logistical services, and then a quest for one with greater cultural similarity that could manage a broader scope of services.

Incorporating interviews with Hans Gutsch, Sandra Fulton, and Karen Monroe, Compaq Computer Corporation; and Mike Brezina, Training & Development Systems.

Part of what lay behind the initial decision to outsource was internal change. In 1995 Compaq refocused its HR function to align with strategic business needs. A concomitant of that decision was to streamline the HR staff. In addition to reducing staff in other HR areas, Compaq decided not to employ trainers and developers, but rather to meet those needs through outsourcing.

The first outsourcing partner they chose was already a valued supplier— a company with proven capability in leadership development, but not in the outsourcing business. The second was a community college with logistical systems in place but with some significant cultural differences. The third is a training and development firm whose co-owner is a former Compaq employee. Compaq also partners with a major university in developing its top-level leaders. While each outsourcing partner has had much to offer, the challenge for Compaq has been to find the one that could meet its rapidly growing requirements in a manner compatible with its culture. As this book goes to press, it appears that the right match now exists. That partnership is still young, however, and virtually all outsourcing partnerships can expect to reinvent their relationship within the first three years.

ABOUT COMPAQ

Founded in 1982, Compaq Computer Corporation is a *Fortune* Global 100 company. Compaq is the second largest computer company in the world and the largest global supplier of personal computers (PCs). Compaq develops and markets hardware, software, solutions, and services, including industry-leading enterprise-computing solutions, fault-tolerant business-critical solutions, networking and communications products, commercial desktop and portable products, and consumer PCs. The company is an industry leader in environmentally friendly programs and business practices. Compaq products are sold and supported in more than 100 countries through a network of authorized Compaq marketing partners. Customer support and information about Compaq and its products are available at http://www.compaq.com.

Clearly, Compaq is making its mark in an extremely competitive industry that has grown and continues to grow at speeds akin to those made famous by another nearby organization—the NASA Space Center. Headquartered in Houston, Texas, where 14,000 of its 79,000 employees work, Compaq is a global company with manufacturing plants in six locations, and sales and marketing organizations in 100 countries.

The highly competitive, fast-paced, and inherently technological nature of the industry dictates some urgency in growing the skills of its employees. In the personal computer sector alone, capacity and speed have doubled every 18 months for more than a decade—remarkable technological accomplishments. At the same time, prices have been driven down regularly, and new competitors with aggressive marketing and sales strategies have put pressure on Compaq and other established companies. As a result, it is essential that Compaq equip its employees to lead through innovation, process improvement, and technology.

Several different groups manage training and development. All of the direct labor training for the manufacturing arena is managed by the HR Development group in Compaq's Manufacturing and Quality organization. Much of this is outsourced to colleges. All technical training is managed at local sites. Other major training and development efforts are directed at the management level. This is the outsourcing story about which this chapter is written.

A HOTHOUSE OF CHANGE

"We've got so much going on that outsourcing training seems like a small thing," says Sandra (Sandy) Fulton, Compaq's manager of worldwide management development. In 1997, that "small thing" ran about 150 training courses for 2,500 employees as well as an orientation program for an additional 2,500 new hires. That was the first year with a new supplier, who jumped in during the last quarter. Growth from this base was rapid, but carefully managed.

Today, Compaq utilizes multiple training and development suppliers, but outsources the administration of most of its management training to Training & Development Systems (TDS). This firm's responsibilities include contracting with other vendors, hiring and supervising trainers, developing new courses, scheduling, registration, and billing for training at its Houston headquarters and other U.S. facilities. In addition, Compaq contracts directly with Harvard University for Lessons in Leadership, a customized program for Compaq's executives and high-potential leaders. Together, the two outsourcing arrangements allow Compaq's corporate staff to remain focused on strategic issues.

The outsourcing of training was not such a small thing when Sandy joined Compaq in 1997. In fact, it was consuming 70 percent of her work time in ways that were not productive. She was spending precious days in fire fighting. So she changed suppliers—twice—in an outsourcing process that began before her tenure.

THE DECISION TO OUTSOURCE

Hans Gutsch became senior vice president for human resources and environment in 1994. "For our first 10 or 11 years, we had the traditional thinking and approach of a fast-growing company," he says. "We operated traditional classroom training with our own Compaq trainers and offered many programs to select from. We were geared to developing or enhancing skills. When I came over, we assessed the whole HR function and aligned ourselves with the business. We now look toward future requirements based on our overall business plan, and focus on people development as well as skills training."

As a result, Compaq now diagnoses and assesses its employees' needs in relation to defined competency models, and then delivers training that is targeted at desired outcomes. They put particular emphasis on the future and on equipping future leaders to meet the company's challenges. Overall, there are fewer programs, but of higher quality, all managed by a small but very influential group. "This is not a completely new philosophy," says Gutsch, "but we have really executed it."

The change is dramatic, when compared with earlier days. In the late 1980s and early 1990s, Compaq had a large staff of trainers. When the company underwent significant cutbacks during 1992 and 1993, most of those trainers were either dispersed to other positions throughout the company or were laid off. Enter Mike Brezina in 1994, assigned to manage all of the Houston-site management training. He needed to rebuild the program, but how? He reports, "We decided to throw everything on the table and ask what must be done internally. Everything else was up for outsourcing."

Ultimately, the team decided that the strategy must be owned internally, and that more comprehensive training and development must be made available in Houston and worldwide. But they saw no benefit to involving the training and education department in the day-to-day activities. In addition, they forecasted a need for flexibility to meet dynamic training needs. Taken together, these principles formed the rationale and broad framework for outsourcing. This conceptual proposal was presented to senior management. Gutsch agreed: This was the right philosophical fit for his business-driven approach to management development.

SELECTING THE PARTNER

With their priorities clearly in mind, Mike and his team, with consulting help from a major training and education supplier, developed a decision process and plan. They first developed the criteria by which they would select their outsourcing partner. Because HR was now focused on management development in service to business needs, they decided to seek a partner with a depth of experience in that area.

Five other criteria addressed Compaq's decision to hand off the aspects of training that did not need to be handled internally—essentially the capabilities required to design and deliver training. They knew they wanted a partner that had a depth of experience in the training and employee development field. Training coordination and project management directly addressed the logistical side of the outsourcing plan. In addition, they sought research and development capabilities. In so doing, they recognized that an external supplier might well provide a perspective broader than an internal staff would likely deliver, particularly if that partner regularly consulted with other firms. They also sought networking capabilities, knowing that they wanted their prospective partner to connect with other suppliers that could provide expertise in various niches.

Another significant element was cost. In particular, they looked at the value of what they would be receiving in comparison with the proposed fees. And finally, they included an "other" category that would allow them to track special perks or issues that were not on their list of criteria, but might prove important.

With these eight criteria, they established a matrix (see table 6.1), which they used to evaluate seven different organizations: four consulting firms and three colleges or universities.

When the information from the proposals came in, Compaq's first cut was to look at costs. No candidates were eliminated on this basis alone. All of the bids came in within a few thousand dollars per month. That may have been a

Table 6.1. Compaq's Selection Matrix							
	Consulting Firm 1	Consulting Firm 2	Consulting Firm 3	Consulting Firm 4	College/ Univ. 1	College/ Univ. 2	College/ Univ. 3
Mgmt. dev. experience							
Training and dev. exp.							
Training coordination							
Project management							
Research and development							
Networking capabilities							
Budget: value/costs							
Other perks and issues							

factor of how Compaq asked for information: The same number of people days computes to roughly the same number of dollars.

After the financial review, the team compared how the various organizations stacked up on the other criteria. The decision turned out to be remarkably easy. "If we took out management development expertise, we had two or three strong candidates," Mike recalls. "If we added in management development, PDI [Personnel Development Incorporated] jumped off the page."

PDI's particular expertise lay in design, delivery, and assessment of programs from a leadership perspective. One benefit was that they already had a substantial relationship with Compaq. They were deeply involved in growing Compaq's leadership and changing some of its people-development practices. Their projects included developing new competency models, providing individual coaching, offering high-level leadership training, implementing 360-degree feedback processes, and a number of other change-management efforts. Part of PDI's strength in these areas came from its ability to provide best-practice research based on experience with other companies as well as with Compaq. In short, PDI was an excellent consultant with whom Compaq already enjoyed a strong working relationship.

There was one issue, however. PDI was not in the outsourcing business. "They did us a favor," says Mike. "We knew this would not be a long-term solution, but it took us the next step toward where we needed to go."

Partnership with PDI

So the decision was made, the contract written, and the relationship begun. Compaq developed and communicated its expectations for the partnership. They included both the partners' roles and responsibilities and the qualitative aspects of the relationship.

PDI was to take on the coordination of training and orientation, including customization and development of the programs and marketing of them. In addition, they were to evaluate potential training programs. They also were to take on the administration of Compaq's tuition assistance program. They saw an opportunity to create a leadership development center—a library of materials that would be available to company personnel. In addition, because PDI had some existing resources in Germany and Japan, they were well positioned to help Compaq with some of its global training efforts. They helped the company to make connections with training and development suppliers in those countries.

In addition to the work that Compaq contracted PDI to do in their behalf, the Compaq team was very clear about the kind of outsourcing relationship they wanted. They wanted a true partner, one that would be an extension of the corporate group and would be viewed in that way by the company's internal clients. They wanted a seamless transition. And they wanted their partner to be very responsive to internal clients—to see them as their own customers. Because of Compaq's existing relationship with PDI, the team had confidence that these qualitative goals would be achieved.

Compaq's internal training and development group did not shrink as a result of outsourcing. In fact, it grew. They hired consultants to manage the process and brought in permanent administrative staff to handle the day-to-day logistics. In addition, Mike estimates that he spent 30 to 40 percent of his own time on this project. "The consultants we hired were excellent," he says. "They looked at our processes and programs and asked what we could do to make them more streamlined and effective. Based on their efforts, we did make some changes. The ultimate focus for all of us was on achieving Compaq's objectives."

The outsourcing relationship with PDI remained from its inception in 1996 through the spring of 1997. Then a significant change occurred. In January 1997, Mike left Compaq to become a co-owner of TDS (Training & Development Systems).

Lessons Learned: Round 1

Looking back, Mike analyzes what went well and what did not. He attributes the fact that the outsourcing concept still exists to five things his group did well at the outset. First, the decision process was sound. The initial determination to outsource was, and still is, an excellent fit with the company's strategic direction. Outsourcing allows Compaq to focus its employee base on its own core competencies: developing, manufacturing, and marketing computer hardware and software. In addition, Compaq gains real expertise in training and development from a partner with that core competency.

Second, the criteria and selection process also was judicious. It forced Compaq's training and development group to assess where they could add the greatest value internally and what skills and qualities an outside partner could bring. Using a matrix enabled them to compare prospective partners on a fair and impartial basis, and to see the differences among them at a glance. It brought a potentially complicated and confusing task under management.

Third, getting buy-in from senior management was a critical step. Hans Gutsch understood where Compaq needed to go and had a vision of how to reshape the corporate HR group to meet the challenges of the fast-approaching future. Recasting training to better align with employee development was an important part of that. And the decision to outsource as a way of achieving those goals was a critical decision. Such transitions are never easy, and this one was no exception. Particularly in the face of ensuing difficulties, the support of senior management proved to be essential.

A fourth contributor to the success of the concept was effective internal communication. The internal training staff worked with human resource and development (HRD) managers and other clients to communicate the outsourcing concept and rationale. They met on a regular basis before and during the transition and made the business case very clear. Although some of the anticipated questions and resistance occurred, most managers understood the concept and saw its value in the broad perspective.

And last, setting up a short-term pilot at the beginning of the outsourcing relationship was invaluable. Despite the best planning and—in this case—a known supplier, starting a major new relationship is fraught with opportunities for surprise. The Compaq-PDI partners decided to start small, learn from the experience, and then ramp up the project.

On the other side, there were some things Mike would do—and has since done—differently. Probably the biggest reason that Compaq's relationship with PDI did not last lay in the definition of managerial roles. Given PDI's mission and focus, that might not have been avoidable. But had both partners realized the future implications, they might have made a different decision about their outsourcing relationship from the beginning.

"We outsourced pieces, but we did not require PDI to manage their own outsourcing operation," says Mike. "We outsourced the administration but not the management. That was a deficiency." Hiring consultants to manage and employees to help in administration meant that Mike had a substantial managerial job on his hands, beyond simply managing the partnership. And it meant that Compaq was not really out of the training business. As long as the job descriptions remained the same and there was a limit to the growth of the programs, the arrangement was workable. But change did happen—as it always does. And since PDI was not really in control of its own outsourcing project, the arrangement fell apart.

There were some other factors that could have been improved, too. One of the lessons learned was to work more closely with the internal clients to clarify scope of services, requirements, and expectations for both the outsourcing partner and the internal client. While some clients used such a process, others did not. The result was that while most had a fairly good understanding of the arrangement, not all gave it enthusiastic support.

A related issue is the always-important one of communication. While the training staff had done well at communicating the concept and business case, they had communicated less about tactical details. As Mike recalls, "People in corporate roles tend to think more globally; those in line positions are much more oriented to tactics. They want to know what a typical month will look like—who's doing what, where, and at what price. At the time, we probably did not know all those things. Our experience was too new, and we were still feeling our way. But we could have helped our clients, our partners, and ourselves more if we had been better equipped to talk about those things."

A Brief Partnership

In the continuing stretch toward globalization and an emphasis on development rather than on training, Compaq redefined the role of the training and development manager. When Sandy Fulton joined Compaq in April 1997, she was charged with developing a customized competency model, developing the assessment process for Compaq's Global Management Institute, preparing high-potential managers to become future leaders, and managing the domestic training operation. The intent was for her to spend about 80 percent of her time on global processes and 20 percent on the domestic training. For the first half of her first year on the job, the numbers were reversed.

When Sandy arrived, PDI had two employees of their own on site at Compaq and two additional contract employees from another firm. Compaq still owned much of the responsibility and invested far too many people-hours in overseeing training activities. It was clear that Compaq needed to rely on an outsourcing partner that was prepared to take on a larger role in managing its training effort. The partnership needed to be wider and deeper.

So Compaq made a change—but the next choice was short-lived. Compaq chose a junior college, one of the prospective suppliers that had been on the earlier list for consideration. They began their partnership in June and ended it in September. Like PDI, the junior college had a positive existing relationship with Compaq. It appeared that they had appropriate administrative systems that would enable them to take on more of the day-to-day management. The plan they devised together called for the college to begin by taking on some of the training administration. With this base of detailed experience as the starting point, the planned next steps were for them to take on a higher level of management, including identifying and contracting with additional training sources. They never got past phase one.

As it turned out, outsourcing management was not the junior college's core competency any more than it had been PDI's. Once again, this was a good-faith arrangement between organizations that had worked together very well on clearly defined and limited projects, but were not suited to migrate to a different level and scope of partnership. "They were learning as we were. The arrangement was cost-effective in the short term but not managerially effective. Their staff did not have the kind of background necessary to make the decisions we needed to hand off," says Sandy. "It did not work for them, either. They projected that they were going to have to put more resources into the project than they had anticipated." So the arrangement was terminated three months after it began, and a search was once again instituted for the right match.

Partnership with TDS

What was still in place was Sandy's vision of what was needed. "I wanted to find a partner who had expertise in training and development and who also was equipped to own the function for us. I knew that our small HRD group had to focus on global strategic work. We wanted to be involved in strategic issues but leave all of the tactical matters to our partner. Part of that means outsourcing anything to do with the Houston site."

There was one logical place to begin the search for a new partner: TDS. If it could work, it would provide a real shortcut to long-term results. Mike Brezina had the right combination of expertise: He knew training, and he knew Compaq. "When I left Compaq, I did not intend to bid on their business—we never built that into our business plan at TDS, and we never marketed to Compaq. I was happy to help out with their questions after I left, but we were focusing our efforts at TDS on other arenas." Thus TDS hired people to help them achieve their own strategic growth goals. As a result, however, when Compaq did come to them, they had the right kinds of skills to meet their needs.

Mike's phone rang in late September 1997. Sandy Fulton laid out what she was looking for. "We gave Mike our parameters. We would pay TDS to make decisions and manage training; we would manage him. We wanted TDS to work the tactical side; we would work the strategic issues." Could TDS do this? "Yes," Mike answered. When? "We'll start tomorrow," he said. And they did—almost literally. They began October 2, 1997.

The TDS team spent a few days with the junior college before they exited, then jumped in and started to hire people. As Mike had done with PDI, he started this partnership small. This one, however, he planned to grow. Roles were defined. Sandy was to be the training leader. TDS was to be both manager and administrator. The role of Compaq project manager was assigned to Curtis Rice, a gifted, systems-oriented manager with an outstanding work ethic. The firm hired one developer and two administrators to support the project. In addition, they brought in a consultant who serves as a back-up instructor. Mike himself helps Sandy Fulton and Karen Monroe, Compaq's vice president of development and organizational effectiveness, with strategic issues, and sometimes serves as a back-up instructor.

Their strategic plan had four phases: stop the bleeding, attack the root problems, create or improve systems, and grow their base of services. Within a few months, they were already at stage four, while continuing to improve systems. "Our ultimate goal is to become Compaq's strategic partner," says Mike. "We want to provide a very responsive, zero-defect service and take all the issues off of Sandy's plate."

Curtis Rice began by attending to myriad details, thereby regaining the trust of both the vendors and clients. When TDS came on the scene, they found that small but important matters were regularly slipping through the cracks. People were showing up for courses that had been canceled. Vendors who were being paid on the basis of volume were calling participants to confirm their attendance, because they could not rely on class lists. Messages were not returned.

TDS stopped such problems within 30 days. They answered their phone and e-mail messages (e-mail alone had a volume of 200 to 250 per day) within 24 hours. They sent out reminders to course participants one week, rather than one day, in advance. When problems occurred, they addressed them immediately, and probed causes in order to see ways to prevent them from reoccurring. In a short time, they had regained credibility for the training effort.

Next, they moved aggressively to smooth out systems. Compaq had already established quarterly meetings with all key vendors. TDS used these meetings to strengthen the relationships and enable the suppliers to better meet Compaq's needs. TDS reviews the rates, fees, and schedules in an effort to ensure consistency as well as flexibility. They have set up templates for e-mail and streamlined a number of paper processes. They have implemented a system of review for all core courses to ensure that they link to business strategies and values. The overhaul of their registration system has been delayed because Compaq is migrating to PeopleSoft, and it would not be efficient to invest in a new database for a short period of time. But such an overhaul is coming.

As TDS has proved its ability to ensure quality of service and fit with Compaq's needs and direction, Sandy has been delighted to hand off more and more pieces of training management to TDS. She has assigned TDS to take on tuition reimbursement, a program that involves some 1,000 employees and a great deal of paperwork. The Compaq-TDS relationship appears to have built a solid foundation for a long-term outsourcing relationship.

Why It Is Working

In a word, fear! "We felt like we had 30 days to prove we were worthy," says Mike. "We thought if we screwed up, it would be over. Curtis drove the entire team to stay on top of the details. We were—and are—extremely client focused, and we document what we're doing." Within a few months, the panic level had dropped, but the attention to service had not. They had proved themselves and believed they had built enough trust to allow them to work through any issues that might arise.

TDS did, in fact, work as part of Compaq's team. "We needed to change the clients' and suppliers' perception and earn their trust, but at the same time we needed our participation to be seamless. We did not send out anything that said, 'We're here,'" says Mike. The team's e-mail and phone addresses suggested that they were Compaq HRD coordinators—and that was how they behaved. Soon people started seeing a difference. TDS was finding unpleasant surprises up through January of 1998. As problems surfaced, Curtis apologized for them, explained that they were new, and then fixed them. Curtis made it a personal mission to take ownership and relieve Sandy of the problems with which she had been inundated. Initially, the Compaq-TDS staff worked 75 to 80 hours a week.

In addition, the TDS team looked to the long term and tried to be fair in their financial dealings. They had negotiated a monthly fee up front and planned in a monthly review. They documented what they did, but they did not bill for the extras. For instance, Mike taught a course, but rather than add on the day rate for instruction, TDS just absorbed it. It probably meant that TDS did not earn every dollar it could have, but it seemed fair. "Teaching meant that I did not do some other things for Compaq with that time," explains Mike, and it kept the whole relationship out of a nickel-and-dime mentality. Increased stipends would be reserved for major upgrades of service.

As for Sandy, her most immediate measure of success is being met: "My phone doesn't ring!" she exults. Even more important, customer and vendor satisfaction have improved. Schedules are developed and met; rooms are set up; class lists are accurate; supplies are ordered. The headaches have, by and large, gone away. She meets weekly or biweekly with Curtis Rice, sometimes adding on separate budget meetings. Curtis keeps her informed via e-mail and voice mail, so their meeting time is used to make decisions, not review events. By and large, Sandy is finally able to focus on global competencies and future leadership—the job she came to Compaq to do.

CONCLUSION

Now that the Compaq-TDS partnership appears to be solid and growing, it is possible to look back over the first three years of Compaq's outsourcing adventure and extract some lessons. The first is, as suggested in the initial note, that the thematic outsourcing model was not ultimately fulfilled. It may be that such a model can work, but Compaq's experiences with it are not unique. The repeated failures of such relationships necessarily lead to some reservations about the model itself. A number of training managers have reasoned that firms with a particular area of expertise necessarily view a company's training needs through their own bias. Although it would not appear that PDI's management-development "lens" distorted their understanding of Compaq's training and development requirements, the fact is that their real business focus is on their area of expertise—as well it should be. This suggests that while such a firm often fulfills an important and valuable consulting role, it is not typically well suited to partnership. Thus, those who are contemplating a partnership based on the thematic model may do well to ensure that a prospective partner also has appropriate capacity in those transactional factors that are, in fact, likely to have the greatest impact on the success of an outsourcing relationship.

The second lesson that may be extracted from Compaq's experience is that the process of identifying and analyzing vendors is extremely important, but difficult to do well. It would certainly appear that, in its initial search for an outsourcing partner, Compaq followed a thorough and reasonable process in requesting and comparing proposals, but the outcome was questionable. Certainly they would not have chosen the multiple crises they experienced. One possible flaw in their analysis may have been, as noted above, the decision to weight experience in a particular content area higher than the overall capability to manage projects at a detailed level. Or they may have failed to scrutinize these transactional aspects of their prospective partner's capabilities as rigorously as they could have. Adding such other factors as information technology support systems or administrative systems to the decision matrix might have led Compaq to a different decision. Or, their investigation into the projects PDI managed for other customers might have revealed the firm's lack of experience with systems of sufficient depth.

Compaq's second choice of an outsourcing vendor unquestionably suffered from an inadequate investment of effort in the analysis process. Although the information originally gathered was probably not out of date, and although the junior college was already a known quantity, the decision to partner with this organization left Compaq in worse shape than they had been with PDI. It is likely that a more thorough investigation of Tomball's systems and capabilities would have revealed potential problems. Even earlier in the process, however, the addition of "cultural fit" to the list of criteria might have revealed a potential problem. Although there are a few industry-college outsourcing partnerships that work very well, as seen in the Dow-Delta relationship (see chapter 5), the differences between these two cultures are typically so profound as to make a true partnership very difficult.

Another question that surfaces from the Compaq experience is why they entered the original partnership with PDI expecting that it would not be a long-term solution. Initiating an outsourcing partnership requires investing not only time and other resources but also, to a very great extent, the kind of psychological energy associated with a marriage. The new relationship not only affects those managers and administrators of the outsourced tasks but also reaches deeply throughout the company. The outsourcing partner develops relationships with the firm's internal customers. Developing and maintaining such relationships, and the reputations that form their wake, requires time and energy. Furthermore, new relationships often result in changes to systems, and these too affect the customers. Thus it is advisable for both partners to enter an outsourcing relationship with the intent of making it permanent. While it would be naive to assume its permanence, it is equally naive to initiate a partnership without the expectation and determination to make it work for a long time.

Although the learnings cited above come from the difficulties Compaq experienced, perhaps the most important lesson of all is that persistence— smart persistence—pays off. Although it is still too early to claim success for the Compaq-TDS partnership, it has the earmarks of a winner. The cultures fit; the transactional needs are now well defined and the right kinds of efforts are being made to meet them; and growth is being implemented in phases. The turmoil Compaq experienced early on is not unique. What is remarkable is their determination to make outsourcing work. The biggest factors in their ultimate success are vision and persistence. By maintaining a clear vision of what was needed, Compaq made the difficult but ultimately correct decisions to terminate the partnerships that were not working. By adding perseverance to that vision, they are now creating one that may turn out to be among industry's most successful.

One final note: Because they have been willing to share their experiences and insights candidly, they have made an important contribution to the body of outsourcing information that may help others walk a smoother path. For this, everyone should be grateful.

7

MULTIPARTNER OUTSOURCING: KAISER PERMANENTE'S APPROACH

7

This chapter provides a look at two aspects of outsourcing, in particular. First is the multipartner model, which is being increasingly used by large service firms. Kaiser Permanente was among the first companies to develop such an approach—and the use of multiple partners was not part of their original plan. That brings us directly to the second point: The process of developing successful outsourcing partnerships is often a crooked path. Kaiser Permanente's experiences provide an excellent opportunity to observe some of the twists and turns such a project can take, and to learn from them. Like Compaq, Kaiser Permanente held fast to a vision of what outsourcing could be and then made it happen, despite some serious problems and frustrations. Their resolve and creative problem solving are two key character traits frequently needed to make outsourcing work.

OVERVIEW

As this book goes to press, Kaiser Permanente (KP), the world's largest not-for-profit health maintenance organization, is in the midst of a major transformation. In response to the fundamental changes that recently have swept through the entire U.S. health care industry, Kaiser Permanente has recently mounted some major organizational changes designed to ensure the highest levels of customer service, meet regulations, cut costs, and retrofit its structure to address the needs of this dramatically altered environment.

Incorporating interviews with Kathryn Arbour, former director of human resources shared services, and Madeline Fassler, director of training, Kaiser Permanente of Northern California.

One central locus for change is California, KP's largest entity. The northern California and southern California divisions merged into a single statewide division in 1997. Because each KP geographic unit operates as a separate but cooperating entity, the process of shaping two organizations into a single division requires a huge amount of change. But as we have seen with Quest and Compaq, change has become a constant in many organizations. In its wake, company leaders must deal with both predictable and unpredictable challenges in order to adjust corporate systems quickly and smoothly. Many look to outsourcing as a solution that provides flexibility in such an environment. The human resources (HR) leaders at Kaiser Permanente of Northern California, about which this chapter is written, had recently established a new structure for training and learning that could accommodate growth. Nonetheless, the new organization is once again experiencing the turbulence that inevitably accompanies a merger of this magnitude.

At the heart of the Kaiser Permanente story is the organization's size, culture, and complexity. This is a huge service organization. As a health care provider, it is heavily regulated and requires not only a wide array of highly specific training but also accurate documentation of it. A large portion of its huge workforce is represented by collective bargaining, and the physicians themselves form another very powerful entity within the company. And like all organizations, the very structure of KP reflects its history and culture. In this case, small, somewhat autonomous units grew into a multifaceted, immense organization. In recent years, they have felt the pressures of competition and increased public and governmental scrutiny that have affected their entire industry.

The question, then, is how such an organization moves out of its past into a lean, competitive organization. In particular, how was it to transform its diverse, local training and education efforts into an efficient, effective companywide training and education system? The answer Kaiser Permanente devised was to outsource, and to use more than one partner, each equipped with a particular core competency that serves one or more of KP's large-scale needs. What they have developed is probably the most intricate model of outsourcing currently in use anywhere. The process of finding the right configuration of partnerships to meet their unique organizational needs has been marked by enormous energy—some starts, stops, changes in direction, major organizational changes, and more than a little anguish. The architects of the new KP Learning Works organization doggedly kept peeling back the layers to discern their company's needs, prospective suppliers' capabilities, and structures that could create a workable system. The result of their persistence is a complex, multipartner system that yielded 95 percent satisfaction levels among its customers within the first year of operation.

ABOUT KAISER PERMANENTE

The Kaiser Permanente Medical Care Program is currently the largest, non-profit, prepayment health care plan in the United States. "An integrated health delivery system, KP organizes and provides or coordinates members' care, including preventive care such as well-baby and prenatal care, immunizations, and screening devices, hospital and medical services, and pharmacy services." As a whole, KP provides comprehensive medical and hospital services to more than 9.1 million voluntarily enrolled members in seven divisions over 19 states and the District of Columbia. It encompasses a whole set of interconnected organizations, including Kaiser Foundation Health Plan, Incorporated, and several subsidiaries: Kaiser Foundation Hospitals, the Permanente Medical Groups, Group Health Cooperative of Washington, and Community Health Plan of New York. Together, these organizations employ more than 10,000 full-time physicians representing every specialty, and more than 90,000 nonphysician technical, administrative, and clerical employees.

"The organization that is now Kaiser Permanente began at the height of the Great Depression with a single inventive young surgeon and a 12-bed hospital in the middle of the Mojave Desert. When Sidney A. Garfield, M.D., looked at the thousands of men involved in building the Los Angeles Aqueduct, he saw an opportunity. He borrowed money to build Contractors General Hospital... and began treating sick and injured workers." Without insurance, however, many patients had no way to pay for these services. Because Doctor Garfield refused to turn away sick or injured workers, in no time, the hospital's expenses were far exceeding its income. At this point, Harold Hatch, an engineer-turned-insurance-agent, "suggested that the insurance companies pay Doctor Garfield a fixed amount per day, per covered worker, up front. This would solve the hospital's immediate money troubles, and at the same time enable Doctor Garfield to emphasize maintaining health and safety rather than merely treating illness and injury. Thus 'prepayment' was born."

The first big expansion of this concept came when Henry Kaiser sought health care for workers in the largest construction project in history, the

Grand Coulee Dam. He enrolled 6,500 construction workers and their families. Doctor Garfield recruited a team of doctors to work in a prepaid group practice. The next expansion came as the United States entered World War II. The Kaiser Shipyards in Richmond, California, were commissioned to build aircraft carriers and other military vessels. This time, Henry Kaiser sought to address the health care needs of 30,000 workers. President Franklin Roosevelt intervened and enabled Doctor Garfield, already scheduled for active duty, to be released from his military obligation specifically to organize and run a prepaid group practice for these workers. Thus the innovative medical system came to the San Francisco Bay Area and formed an association with Henry J. Kaiser that would embed itself in the organization.

After the war, the number of shipyard employees dropped from its high of 90,000 to just 13,000 in a matter of months. But Doctor Garfield and Henry Kaiser wanted the plan to continue. So in 1945, the Permanente Health Plan officially opened to the public. In 10 years, enrollment surpassed 300,000 members in northern California, largely through the support of two unions, the International Longshoremen and Warehousemen Union, and the Retail Clerks Union. Thus the organization now known as Kaiser Permanente was born. KP is still a working partnership of two organizations: the not-for-profit Kaiser Foundation Health Plan and Hospitals, and the Permanente Medical Groups (http:www.kaiperm.org/about, 4/25/98).

Today, KP still operates as a decentralized organization. The majority of day-to-day decisions regarding the management of health care services and facilities are made at the regional level through a structure of separate but closely associated organizations.

Before merging with the southern California division in 1997, Kaiser Permanente of Northern California provided care to more than 2.4 million health-plan members. Its 35,000 employees provided services through 16 medical centers and 14 outpatient medical offices—each with considerable autonomy. In 1995, however, the company experienced a downturn in business. Faced with a loss of market share, company leaders undertook a fresh analysis of the organization. One of the compelling needs they addressed was to become more customer focused. They redefined their understanding of the customer to include not only patients but also purchasers of health plans. Based on this revised definition, they redrew the lines of the organization according to customer groups. The result was the creation of seven customer service areas, each containing four or five medical centers. The company was thus organized into small business units.

The implications of such a change were huge. Previously, each medical group had managed its own organization, including the HR function. Under this decentralized structure, each unit had its own unique approach to recruitment, training, benefits, labor consultation, and other HR services. The result was, not surprisingly, that an enormous amount of duplication and redundancy existed within this single division of Kaiser Permanente.

CHANGING THE STRUCTURE FOR LEARNING

Bernard Tyson, assistant regional manager and vice president of human resources, saw the fragmentation within his division, and had a vision for the future. Tyson determined to restructure the entire HR function into a single, centralized, efficient entity. Kathryn Arbour was brought into Kaiser Permanente in 1994 to take one of several leadership roles in this organizational change process. She was initially assigned to work with teams in implementing the new business structure. Her next responsibility was to lead a task force on the redesign of human resources. The goal of the redesign was for this function to better support the new customer-focused organization. One fundamental premise for the new HR was that it should have a single budget that was essentially, as Kathryn describes, "an investment fund, comanaged like a mutual fund by its stakeholders." The group foresaw such a concept eventually operating for the training effort as well.

As the task force gathered information, it became very evident that training was one of the areas most out of control. This information, and the larger redesign effort, formed the context for changing KP's training system and structure, an effort that Kathryn began to lead in 1995. Two other key players were Madeline (Maddi) Fassler, who now oversees the training organization as director of the newly formed KP Learning Works organization, and Linda Lewis, KP's executive director of human resources.

"At that time, a number of us were attracted to the concept of shared services—an approach that was not yet in widespread use in human resources," says Arbour. "We joined a consortium of other organizations that were using shared services so that we could learn from one another. The basic tenet of the shared-services approach is to segment services in context of economies of scale, areas of expertise, and the role of the business partner. That helped us to rethink training, among other things. We began by looking at all the transactional work: What is everyone doing at the various centers that could be the same?" This idea of bringing consistency to the multiple repetitive transactions that surrounded training became the keystone of their redesign.

One of Kathryn's first steps was to form a group of about 100 people who would serve as advisers on the redesign of the entire human resources function. They mobilized for the first step: assessing the current situation through data collection. Kathryn hired a consulting firm that specialized in performing assessments of this type quickly. They contacted everyone they could identify within the organization who was doing HR or HR-related work. Within four weeks, they had 800 responses that yielded data on multiple facets of the organization. With regard to training, they compiled information on training topics, costs, amount of time employees spent in training, and a list of activities performed by the people contacted. "The results were not surprising," says Kathryn, "but we finally had the information on paper where we could all look at the same thing."

The redundancies and inconsistencies were abundantly clear. A wide range of clinical training, from bedside technique to cardiopulmonary resuscitation (CPR), was interspersed with managerial skills as well as personal skills, such as time and stress management, in a miscellany of training offerings provided by the various operating units. The sources of funding for training came from a variety of budgets. Medical groups, nursing groups, and administrative funds were all tapped to pay training bills. As a result, it was difficult to understand exactly how much KP of Northern California, as an entity, was paying for training. Another outcome of this budgeting structure was that the pricing was replete with inconsistencies. Time management, for example, came in at anywhere from pennies to $100 per person, and costs for identical certifications ranged from $25 to $125.

With this body of information in hand, the team undertook the next step in its information-gathering process. This was to conduct a series of interviews with key stakeholders on their level of satisfaction with the current training programs. Again, not surprisingly, the satisfaction level was low. "We were spending a lot of money on programs that were not delivering value," Kathryn reports. In addition, the process efficiency was at a very low level. "We were generating vast quantities of paper and underutilizing technology— a practice that's fairly typical of medical organizations."

Another important piece of information emerged from the studies. When researchers tried to identify all the staff members who had something to do with training—some 400 people—they discovered that few had formalized training backgrounds. This raised some questions about whether KP had the internal resources it would need in order to build a training organization.

Once the data came back from the surveys and interviews, the 100 advisers gathered for three days, an amount of time that in and of itself represented a remarkable demonstration of commitment to the change process. The group had three goals. The first was to validate the data, which, by and large, they were able to do. The second was to determine what the data suggested about KP's future direction in training. The third was for the advisers to identify their own individual interests and passions, and for them to begin self-selecting to serve on a task force for the next phase of redesign.

From that powerful, idea-packed beginning, the task force pushed ahead. Work groups were formed and met regularly. Each group defined deliverables and milestones. In addition, each tried to identify potential barriers to success and suggest ways to eliminate them. From these multiple, rich discussions, the concept of a centralized service center emerged. This centralized service center would provide shared services to all of the operating units in its service area. With what proved to be excellent foresight, the group envisioned this service center to be statewide. Such a concept had multiple benefits. A centralized operation had the potential to dramatically reduce redundancies, reduce costs through consolidated purchasing power, and at the same time improve quality. In addition, by eliminating many redundant tasks, KP would be able to make some reductions in head count. After making a very sound business case for this new structure, Arbour and the teams spent most of 1996 implementing it.

THE SHAPE OF THINGS TO COME

The proposed new consolidated training-learning organization would have centralized management in the form of the statewide service center. Under that umbrella, they would administer training programs organized into three broad categories. The first was core services: compliance-based clinical training as well as a group of other courses that were seen as essential to day-to-day operations. The second was training to address individual needs: courses such as time management, stress management, communication skills, and others aimed at improving the basic skills individual workers need to be effective on the job. The third category was oriented to the future. This body of training would address whatever might be needed to help KP remain competitive. For example, every physician might learn a second language, or those involved in records management might receive training in new computer systems implemented for centralized recordkeeping.

As the research had revealed, however, Kaiser Permanente did not have the internal expertise to design, deliver, and administer its own training. The team thought that the best approach was for the service center to outsource all of the transactional work—such items as registration, billing, and reporting. The consolidation and outsourcing of these logistical aspects of the training operation were essential to the mission of improving both the quality and efficiency of this area. In addition, the team wanted to outsource a fair amount of routine and core training programs—essentially the first two categories of training. Outsourcing the logistics and these subject areas would enable them to focus a small internal group on identifying and addressing the more strategic future needs that were more deeply embedded in the organization. With that broad structure in mind, they began their search for "a single all-knowing partner."

They began the process by putting out a request for proposal (RFP). This RFP thoughtfully and rigorously outlined its needs and provided a clear and honest picture of KP's organizational culture. It also made clear the kind of in-depth partnership KP was seeking.

Kaiser Permanente had established prior relationships with a number of vendors who were already delivering a range of services. Many of these stepped forward and expressed their interest in developing a larger partnership. In addition, KP sought proposals from several other firms that had experience in outsourcing relationships with other corporations. Once the proposals came in, KP undertook a careful selection process. They identified seven contenders that likely had sufficient capacity to undertake such a project. The team reviewed the proposals carefully, and developed a short list. The next task was to conduct extensive interviews, first by phone and then in person, with several firms whose capabilities and experiences appeared to provide the right fit with KP's needs and culture.

From these, they selected Forum Group, a major training and change-management company, and a supplier with whom they had already done a lot of business. The decision was made in part because of Forum's large size; KP was certain it would require a big organization to undertake a project as large as theirs. Forum had proved itself with two other large firms in what appeared to be similar partnering situations. In addition, Forum had worked closely with KP in some strategic work involving large-scale culture change. Thus they knew the organization well in an area that provided context for future training pieces. It was expected that Forum would subcontract various pieces of the work, but would essentially serve as the managers of most of KP's training operation. KP saw the potential for leveraging buying power based on not only the size of their own operation but also that of the partnering organization. It appeared at first that this outsourcing arrangement would bear fruit.

Initially, both partners were delighted. Almost immediately, however, the project ran into trouble. The first issue that surfaced was a timing and process issue. KP came to the table with a real sense of urgency to get certain categories of training off the ground quickly; they had a mandate to implement training through this new arrangement within a three-month window. This timeline was not negotiable. Corporate funding had been rearranged. People had been let go. Internal customers were waiting. There was a lot of pressure—some of it self-imposed—to move quickly.

"Forum wanted to step back and examine whether the categories of training KP wanted to launch were of strategic value. They thought that the only right thing to do was start from square one and conduct their own needs assessment and analysis. They were doing the right thing as our consultant to try to align our programs with our strategy and to try and avoid potential problems," Kathryn reflects. "However, we had already confronted those issues about eight months previously and realized that we didn't have a way out of it. In order to gain credibility, we knew we were going to have to deliver on some nonstrategic things simply because our constituents really wanted them. We had already made the compromise. But that didn't fit with Forum's mental model and approach."

A second major issue was the broad range of activities that KP wanted to hand off—everything from the detailed logistics of enrollment tracking systems to brokering large chunks of training, with delivery, design, learning consulting, and many other pieces in between. As Maddi Fassler explains, "Forum clearly had expertise in some of these areas, but were at that point fledgling in some others." In the area of subcontracting, for instance, it turned out that KP had more information about prospective partners in certain areas of expertise than Forum did, and in some cases, already-established relationships.

The third big issue was cost. Forum proposed a sizable organization, which they thought they needed in order to manage the whole process and a number of other suppliers. The sheer size of this organization meant that it would be costly. KP countered with a leaner proposal.

"As all these pieces emerged, it just became more evident to all of us that we needed to be more networked, at least in the beginning," says Kathryn. For two months, the partners went back and forth. Ultimately, they could not agree. KP made the painful decision to abandon the single-partner concept and seek several partners, each with a particular area of expertise that matched one or more of KP's defined major needs. In retrospect, Arbour reflects, "Had we been farther along, we probably could have handed the training off to a single, well-equipped firm." But the timing just was not right, so they regrouped and plunged in again. Still deeply valued for its strengths, its values, and its compatibility with KP, Forum was retained as one of the partners in the new arrangement.

KP'S MULTIPARTNER OUTSOURCING ARRANGEMENT

What KP soon developed was a multipartner outsourcing arrangement. This is now managed by their own Central Service Center, which includes KP Learning Works, along with several HR transactional areas (see figure 7.1).

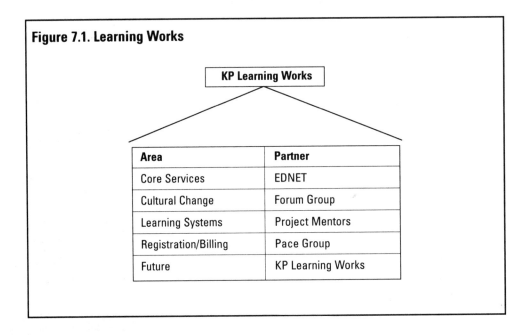

Figure 7.1. Learning Works

KP Learning Works

Area	Partner
Core Services	EDNET
Cultural Change	Forum Group
Learning Systems	Project Mentors
Registration/Billing	Pace Group
Future	KP Learning Works

KP Learning Works became the nerve center that Kathryn and Maddi had originally envisioned outsourcing. With the recent merger in place, this organization has been challenged not only to start up the new outsourcing relationships but also to expand the services statewide.

The current partnerships are structured to address two of the three content areas identified earlier: core services and cultural change. In addition, KP sought an outsourcing solution to one of its critical functional areas: the registration, billing, and reporting process. And most recently, they added a relationship that supplements the course offerings with complete systems. As they had originally intended, they have retained future planning internally.

The core services—the clinical training for the medical and paramedical staff—are being delivered largely by EDNET, a network of community colleges in the Bay Area. Many of these courses teach technical processes that are required for certification. Their portfolio includes not only traditional classroom training but also a number of online courses—a real benefit for a medical service organization where scheduling is driven by clinical needs, and releasing a group of similarly skilled employees all at the same time is highly problematic. In addition, EDNET is able to provide a certain number of proprietary classes, such as Zenger-Miller, which they are licensed to offer. Because they have geographically dispersed classrooms and instructors, they can provide such courses more efficiently than KP, even though KP is licensed to offer many of the same courses.

Forum Group is providing services that reflect one of their core competencies, large-scale cultural change. For instance, as Maddi Fassler explains, "We have defined competencies and linked these to total compensation. So Forum has been able to help us design programs that we're using to build those competencies." For instance, customer service is one of KP's key strategies. Forum can design, develop, and deliver programs that help KP develop an organizational culture with behaviors that consistently reflect this way of doing business.

Project Mentors is the most recent addition to KP's alliance of partners. Project Mentors's niche at KP is their expertise in total learning systems. They work on a project basis, supplying everything from consulting for sponsors who are considering launching projects, to classes on skills such as project management and the software tools that support it, to CD-ROM tutorials and supporting materials. "We were not looking to buy off-the-shelf courses, but looking for a company that can support learning programs from beginning to end," says Maddi. "They can help us to get leadership buy-in, create a model where everybody speaks the same language, and then implement and support it from every angle. For instance, looking at work as projects to be managed is a major culture shift for us. This is highly leveraged learning, and Project Mentors has the multifaceted capability to help us make it happen."

The fourth major partner in KP's alliance is the Pace Group, a subsidiary of Sylvan Learning. The major competency that Pace brings to KP is the capacity to handle virtually all of the logistics: online and telephone registration, tracking, billing, tuition reimbursement, and report generation.

In the heavily regulated health care industry, documentation of individual enrollment in, and completion of, courses is a critical need. Without proof that employees have taken the required numbers of courses, regulatory agencies can deduct points from the provider's certifications. Thus it is critical to Kaiser Permanente to have meticulous records of enrollment. In addition, tracking costs in an efficient manner is a real business need.

Pace was able to provide the right solution at the right time. When the KP partnership was formed, Pace had recently merged with Sylvan Learning. They had an established call center, billing, and registration systems, and online capability. By calling a toll-free 888 number, any California KP employee can register for a host of core programs. On a quarterly basis, Pace updates its database with KP's upcoming training programs. In addition, Pace is able to transfer its database of registrations to the central database at Kaiser Permanente, thus facilitating the regulatory reporting requirements.

The Pace system offers enormous opportunities for expansion. The first addition to the original plan was to include some of the physicians' programs. This presented a new challenge. Because KP's bylaws require that the physician information be kept confidential, Pace had to re-create its database using only the physician's name and a record number for tracking purposes. This has not been without glitches, but the system has undergone continuous improvement, and now more and more physician-based programming is being entered into the database. In addition, Pace is able to supply some contract instructors, and some generic individual-skills courses: communications, listening, and meeting management.

As for the future, the California merger has become the major current project. KP Learning Works has necessarily placed the regulatory requirements at the top of their list of priorities, and that pragmatic need is now consuming most of the group's time. As a result, the broader philosophical role that Kathryn Arbour originally envisioned for this group has been put on hold. As the immediate needs come under management, KP Learning Works may ultimately be able to refocus on learning. As she suggested early in the redesign process, "Training is definable; learning is more amorphous. To create a learning focus in the culture requires a more collaborative effort on the job." The differing philosophies that have evolved in the northern and southern regions will need to be discussed and debated. Each region has its own philosophy embedded in its current management approach and culture. While the north has developed its organization by building capacity through its managers, the south has driven change through an organizational development approach. In the future, however, learning consultants may approach organizational change through a learning perspective. But it will take time to move the organization from its current training approach to one that is driven more by learning.

MANAGING THE ALLIANCE OF PARTNERS

All four outsourcing partnerships, plus the self-assigned task of preparing for the future, are managed through a single, lean, centralized staff. The KP Learning Works organization is composed of a director and a team of senior learning consultants. Each consultant has a dual set of responsibilities. The first is to provide expertise in a particular specialty. In this role, each expert serves as the team's internal consultant. For example, one person has expertise in customer service, another in coaching and team effectiveness, another in leadership and management development, another in mandatory programs, another in managing external relationships, and so forth. The other responsibility is to a particular constituency. For example, the consultant with special expertise in managing external relationships in fact provides guidance in managing the major partners in a way that provides maximum economic benefit and minimum confusion to the customers and users. The consultant whose expertise is in coaching and team effectiveness works with patient care leaders and the nursing staff. The expert in mandatory programs is assigned to work with the operations support department, a group that includes engineering, environmental services, and health and safety.

By having individual consultants work closely with leaders in the various constituencies, the consulting team as a whole can stay connected to trends and future needs as perceived by the people who are providing care and services throughout the organization. By sharing this information at the corporate level, they are able to plan appropriately, investing their resources in those areas that confer the greatest benefit to the organization over the long term.

Thus a structure is in place that provides a depth of expertise in needed areas. Ultimately, such an organization will be able to focus a part of its energy on planning for the future. For now, however, Learning Works director Maddi Fassler is managing all four outsourcing partnerships, utilizing the expertise of her internal consultants as needed. Each of the outsourcing partners also has a single person assigned to the role of managing the KP relationship. In addition, KP has a coordinator assigned to handling logistics at each geographic site.

For now, KP Learning Works is staying abreast of understanding its internal customers' needs by frequent mail and telephone surveys. The data derived from these feeds into the planning process for the next phase. Thus a lot of programming is driven by individual needs. At some future point, KP Learning Works may expand the scope of its planning process to take a broader view of learning in the context of organizational needs. One structure that has been considered for this broader-scope planning process is the formation of the Learning Board. As an advisory group of leaders from all parts of the California KP organization, such a group could help KP Learning Works understand what learning experiences the organization can provide that will focus on how all KP employees can do their jobs better. For now, however, the focus must remain on meeting today's customer requirements and ensuring the smooth functioning of all systems.

LESSONS LEARNED

The three-year period encompassed by this story reflects an extraordinary amount of growth, change, and organizational learning—and not a little anguish. Kaiser Permanente has done so many things right: a thorough assessment of the situation, a vision of what could be, a forward-looking approach to reshaping the structure for learning, a very thoughtful RFP, a genuine openness to partnering, a great deal of creativity, and utmost integrity in dealing with potential partners as well as their own organization. Nevertheless, their experience has been fraught with truly significant problems.

What is impressive about the California Kaiser Permanente story is not just the huge and still-expanding size of the employee base and training task—although this is monumental. What is most impressive is how well they have learned from their own experiences along the way, and how quickly they have been able to act on what they learned.

In retrospect, Kathryn Arbour believes that the single most important strategy she employed was to gain buy-in throughout the organization at an early stage. Of the 100 advisers who were involved in the early planning, many became deeply invested in the outcome and signed on as very serious partners. Thus the required reorganization had sponsors and champions at many levels and locations throughout KP. These people were able to pave the way in the organization for the changes they helped to shape. Even with such an extensive effort, however, there were some holes. As Maddi Fassler points out, there are places in the organization where some high-level managers did not buy into the new approach. Without a mandate, some local organizations are still competing with the corporate effort.

Communication has been a critical part of KP's planning and implementation effort, as it has in other organizations. Face-to-face meetings were supplemented with frequent use of voice mail and e-mail. The magnitude of the communication effort paralleled the size and scope of the organization and project. Without keeping people informed and involved, the effort would almost certainly have collapsed at one of the junctures.

Probably most impressive of all, however, was KP's willingness to assess the problems it encountered early in the single-partner outsourcing relationship and rapidly shift to a multipartner model. Having charted a course and announced it to the entire company, they had the courage to face the very leaders they had sold on the outsourcing concept and recommend a major course correction. The destination remained unchanged, but the path to get there was substantially altered. This decision was undertaken rapidly but carefully. They quickly assessed what was wrong and what needed to change. Within a few months, they had identified partners, developed contracts, and started the new outsourcing arrangements.

All of this was happening at the same time that two other major change events were occurring. First, the training effort was being completely restructured to a competency-based approach. The competencies were newly defined, so the training organization not only had to sell a new organizational structure to management twice, they did this while selling the entire constituency base on a whole new way of thinking about training and education. Second, the merger with southern California was under way. The implications of this were not only adding huge numbers of internal customers but also engineering the merger of two distinct organizational cultures. As if this were not enough, Kaiser Permanente is also on a fast track for growth in an environment in which the entire health care industry is experiencing tremendous financial pressure. In any organization, changes of such magnitude create the potential for disaster. Thus for the centralized KP Learning Works to be formed and for them to make any progress at all without completely derailing may be just short of miraculous.

Speculating about what aspects of their planning and early implementation could have been improved, Kathryn Arbour points to two areas. The first is the decision process for selecting the vendor. KP's process relied on a thorough RFP and extensive interviewing. Although these focused more on discussions about capabilities and experiences, KP never got deeply into a "show-me" stage. Thus, there were some significant surprises, first with Forum's management approach, and later with Pace's technology. By gaining an early and clear understanding of exactly how each organization would produce the required results—and seeing the evidence for that—KP might have circumvented some problems before the relationships were under way. The second improvement that Kathryn would make in a future project is in the rollout process. As she says, they initially chose a "big bang" approach with Forum, launching a huge effort all at once. Now she believes that staging the implementation incrementally would have enabled them to iron out problems and learn how to work together.

CONCLUSION

KP Learning Works will remain a fascinating project to watch over time. There is an essential tension in the very structure of their model. On one hand, they have developed centralized management for training and development with a lean but complex management structure. On the other, the use of multiple outsourcing partners represents a significant kind of decentralization.

Given the newness of this project and the continuing major change initiative of the merger, the jury is still out on this project. Preliminary measurements indicate that constituents are not entirely happy with the online registration process. This is to be expected, since the initial reaction to such change is almost always resistance. Early feedback on courses suggests that the quality of instruction has gone up. But local managers who were accustomed to exercising control and could "add on a section of a course by walking next door," as Maddi says, are less satisfied. There continue to be adjustments and changes; the nature of any organization is that it will continue to change.

The strongest reasons for the probability of KP Learning Works' success are the people who have shepherded and continue to shepherd this complex entity. Kathryn Arbour's vision and leadership in creating the architecture provided a foundation on which her colleagues were well able to build, subsequent to her leaving KP. Maddi Fassler and her colleagues have managed to maintain the big picture throughout, and continue to do so. They anticipated the need for growth and thus were able to accommodate the demands placed on them by the merger. The outsourcing partnerships they have formed appear to be serving their needs. They still hold fast to the vision of shaping a learning organization, and have devised a structure—the Learning Board—to help them achieve yet another significant organizational change. They are realizing more each day, however, that change must be managed incrementally. While they push forward aggressively, their eagerness has been tempered with the wisdom they have gained from the past several years' experiences. The future will continue to hold challenges, and KP is equipped to meet them.

References

Kaiser Permanente. About Kaiser Permanente. Cited 25 April 1998. http://www.kaiperm.org/about.

8

SELECTIVE OUTSOURCING: A LONG-TERM PARTNERSHIP FOR TRAINING ADMINISTRATION

8

*O*ver time, solid partnerships mature. This chapter describes one
of the longest-lived outsourcing partnerships in the area of
training, education, and development. Like the majority of training
partnerships today, CCFL/Corning provides administrative services. Unlike many, however, this one reflects a depth of integration
and flexibility that truly define the concept of "seamless." This chapter reveals Corning's process in arriving at the decision to outsource, some of the major changes that have occurred in the partnership, and some key factors that have made it possible for these
two organizations to work together so successfully.

OVERVIEW

This version of the CCFL/Corning story begins at the end, with how this partnership is working 11 years after its inception. Today, Corning Incorporated
purchases the design, development, and delivery of its training products from
CCFL (College Center of the Finger Lakes). This relationship, dating from
1987, goes far beyond the normal customer-supplier interaction. Corning's
internal training and education function, now called Human Resources Effectiveness, retains responsibility for guiding the corporate strategic leadership
in the effective use of training, and specifically for developing the content of
three training areas: supervisor effectiveness, orientation, and senior leadership development. The combination of these two functions—Corning's strategic leadership for companywide initiatives plus CCFL workshops—is called
CCFL/Corning. This new structure is the result of outsourcing. How and why
did this take place at Corning? What have the results been so far?

ABOUT CORNING

Corning traces its origins to Amory Houghton's 1851 purchase of an interest in a Cambridge, Massachusetts, glass company and the 1864 acquisition of the Brooklyn (New York) Flint Glass Company. Four years later, the operations were transferred upstate to Corning and renamed Corning Flint Glass Company. Among the company's early products were thermometer tubing, pharmaceutical glassware, railroad signal glass, and tableware blanks. The company was incorporated in 1875 as Corning Glass Works and was renamed Corning Incorporated in 1989 to reflect its growing diversification. With a long history of innovation and expertise in glass and ceramic technologies, Corning has played a key role in such major technical advances as the electric lightbulb, television, optical fiber and components for the telecommunications industry, and thousands of specialized products. Among the measures of its success as an innovator was the National Medal of Technology, awarded by the president in 1994. During the 1980s and early 1990s, the company grew dramatically through expansion into life science and medically related industries, which it spun off as two separate corporations in 1996.

Until 1995, a member of the Houghton family led the company. This family ownership was largely responsible for the company's long-standing emphasis on its values. Its implementation of total quality in 1983 made the company strongly customer focused and process oriented. One manifestation of Corning's success in the quality arena was the Malcolm Baldrige National Quality Award, won by Corning's Telecommunications Products Division in 1995.

Today, Corning is a multinational, worldwide business with a portfolio of some 60,000 products. The company is focused on providing leading-edge technologies for the fastest growing segments of the world's economy. Its family of businesses includes a number of wholly or partially owned companies in many different countries. As its enterprises grow, so does its commitment to enabling employees to develop and fully contribute to the businesses. This translates to a well-developed capability to provide both corporatewide and highly individualized learning opportunities.

CORNING'S DECISION TO OUTSOURCE

In 1987 Corning had a large education and training department, set up along entrepreneurial lines. Each training manager had a great deal of latitude to add courses to the catalog. Many staff members also taught courses. While the department's salaries and benefits were provided by allocated overhead, course fees not only paid for the courses themselves but also provided discretionary funds to the department. As a result, there were some problems. The inventory of training programs was unfocused and uncoordinated. Many courses overlapped in their target audience and skills focus. There was no curriculum in the sense of systematic skills development. While training might at least temporarily increase an individual employee's skills level, there was no perceived increase in organizational skills that could be related to training and education. In addition, there were few internal course design projects, and in fact, few long-term projects of any sort. A training and education staff member's life was divided among instruction, employee counseling, administration, and sales to individual customers.

As Corning changed, the structure of its training and education organization had to change, too. James Houghton, then chairman of the board, had a vision of the corporate culture that demanded major changes in attitudes and actions. To effect these changes, the leadership made a tremendous commitment to training. The outline of the program was clear. Corning was to develop a set of core strategic skills as an organization. Employees were required to spend 5 percent of their work time in training. At the same time, the business leaders were calling for greater cost-effectiveness in the training effort. The challenge was to increase both quality and quantity with less investment.

The corporate leadership called in a new training and education team to manage the implementation of this change. It was faced with seemingly contradictory directives. The team wanted to go to a core emphasis on organizational change. They were committed to keeping the budget flat while at the same time providing a much more extensive program. They saw a need for additional skills courses to meet the 5 percent requirement. Furthermore, they wanted to provide individual counseling on training needs, and to develop and administer distance education. Given the current environment, the corporate training staff had to take immediate action and make an immediate impact. They needed to meet the new requirements, and they needed a new image internally. They could not meet these goals by introducing services in a piecemeal fashion. The leadership team wanted to remedy the "mile wide–inch deep" reputation they had acquired over the years—and do it quickly.

The solution they arrived at was to outsource, or "partner," as it was called then. The objective was to focus the training group on the core activities required for this new strategic approach and to send the rest of the activities to an external organization. This revolutionary approach drew a mixed response. The three primary internal customer groups offered varied—and conflicting—initial reactions to the idea of outsourcing major components of the training function.

Upper management was enthusiastic. From a corporate perspective, they saw opportunities to trim costs and to develop a company, and training department, that functioned more effectively. And since they were at a distance from the day-to-day operation of the training and education function, they were comfortable with the decision to outsource. They had realized that this would not be a "business as usual" situation from the outset and were willing to live with some difficult changes at the operational level.

The second customer group to react was the training staff. A fair-sized segment of this group reacted to the outsourcing decision with a mixture of personal fear and professional concern. Many said, in essence, "No one can do this kind of training but us. You are talking about our jobs; what else will we do?" As with the corporate leaders' response, this was an understandable reaction. A few of the education professionals had a different, two-part response. They saw a personal and departmental advantage to using outside resources for some parts of the training and education function. They said, however, "You can do the commodity stuff, but you'll never be able to touch certain areas."

The third customer group was the company's internal customers for training. Their reaction was indifference to the source of supply. They said, "As long as it costs less and works, I don't care who does what. I just want the same or better service with reduced cost and overhead allocation."

CORNING'S REASONS FOR OUTSOURCING

The Corning experience encompasses the classic reasons for outsourcing. Like most firms, Corning wanted to accomplish the following things:

- *Reduce Costs.* The logic was this: An external organization that focused exclusively on training and had multiple customers would be able to achieve economies through its more efficient cost structure.

- *Add Expertise.* Again, in looking beyond its own walls, the company was looking for a partner with best-in-class performance, since that would the supplier's core activity.

- *Provide Comprehensive Services.* Corning realized that a partner often could bring a cluster of related activities.
- *Achieve Continuous Improvement.* Since the external partner would focus on training, keeping up on the latest developments and making existing offerings better would be essential for its existence.
- *Sharpen Their Strategic Focus.* The activities to be retained after the outsourcing activity took place would become the life of the unit. The notion was that this group could perform better with fewer distractions.

Of these five objectives, the most important was the decision to sharpen its strategic focus. Corning affirmed its decision to lead organizational change through training and education and prepared to ramp up these efforts. Cost reduction, or at least control and stabilization of costs, was the secondary strategic objective.

CHOOSING CORE COMPETENCIES

In retrospect, it is difficult to argue with Corning's reasons for outsourcing; everyone wants better performance and lower costs. The difficulties appear, however, with the nuts-and-bolts decisions concerning which activities to outsource and which to retain. In deciding what to outsource, Corning's business leaders had helped tremendously by identifying the cultural core of the company. Translating this into an operational decision both at a company and departmental level was a major task in and of itself. The internal training organization asked some questions that had no easy answers: What is it that we do better than anyone else? What do we do so well that we could sell this product or service on the open market and people would buy it? Where do we achieve best-in-class status? They also asked the opposite questions: Where are we a commodity producer? Where are we adding little value to the production process?

The Corning training and education group decided that innovation and new product development, cultural diversity, leadership development, high-performance work teams, and quality were their core competencies. These would, therefore, be kept internal. Training in these areas would be Corning-specific, deployed companywide, supported by performance systems, and taught to intact work groups. These efforts were to advance the high-impact cultural change as identified by the chairman and leadership team. Accordingly, they had mandated these courses as training requirements. With the focus on these initiatives internally, the "commodity" courses could be re-sourced externally. Commodities were defined as individual skills courses and included their delivery and logistics. Skills courses included Presentations, Statistical Process Control, and Business Writing. Shortly after the corporate group made this decision, the group that managed quality decided that content, not delivery, formed the real "core-of-the-core." Therefore, the delivery of courses in Quality was added to the outsourcing package.

CHOOSING A PARTNER

Having selected the courses and functions to be outsourced, the next task was to choose a vendor. Corning examined several possible partners including colleges and universities, consulting firms, and community organizations. Their criteria for the partner were a mixture of hopes and fears. They wanted a group that specialized in training and education, knew the company well, would be acceptable to users of training services, and would fit both the company environment and the new training philosophy. This external organization would need to be able to provide leadership, but not have a separate agenda that conflicted with that of the new corporate training and education group.

The team identified the following seven specific criteria against which potential outsourcing partners would be judged:

1. *Stability.* As a manufacturing firm, Corning was experienced in dealing with suppliers. Thus they understood how important it would be not to risk having this organization slip away. The possibilities of that scenario are pretty grim: chaos that affects the workplace, plus the time and expense required to find a new supplier.

2. *Experience.* The Corning team knew that this is among the most important predictors that a supplier will be able to provide the services needed and provide them well. A depth of experience with long-term customers usually suggests that a supplier not only has met requirements but also has grown with the inevitable changes.

3. *Financial Success.* The training team understood that success should be profitable. Thus they decided to look for an outsource

company that had a record of making money—not by gouging clients, but by undertaking an enterprise and making it work.

4. *Documented Processes.* As a company deeply committed to quality, Corning knew that the use of documented processes supports consistent, effective, efficient performance.

5. *Recruiting Capability.* Corning knew that over the course of a long-term relationship, personnel would change. In order to ensure consistency and quality, the firm they chose would have to be able to replace or supplement staff with qualified people.

6. *Systematic Training for Its Own Staff.* The training team, more than any other group in the company, understood the importance of developing staff through systematic training. Not only is this necessary to bring new people up to speed, it is also essential to ensure employees' continued growth.

7. *Cultural Similarities.* Corning was among the first companies to begin talking about its corporate culture. They had articulated their own values and had a strong sense of how they worked together. Thus they knew how important it would be for a vendor to be able to fit into their environment. A clash of cultures would have the potential to cause serious disruption with the very customers the training and education function was trying to serve through this new arrangement. They identified trust as the most important single element of the partnership.

A project team was formed specifically to carry out the vendor selection process. The team included a senior manager, logistics coordinators, and a project manager. The selection process took about three months and involved a concise request for proposal, interviews, references, and a fair amount of intuition. The result of their work was to select CCFL as Corning's partner in training and education.

Why would this organization, in particular, be of interest to Corning? There were several reasons, in addition to meeting the criteria mentioned previously. In contrast to colleges, CCFL has no faculty and no permanent programs—an advantage in this situation. It is a design, development, and marketing organization that draws in additional project resources as needed. This results in flexibility and rapid response. In addition, in contrast to consulting firms, it is a not-for-profit organization—another advantage. This means that their mission is defined in terms of its service rather than its profitability, resulting in a clear focus on customer needs and cost savings. CCFL also had a third advantage over other prospective training providers: It was already a supplier. For years, they actually had competed with Corning's own training group for company dollars. Its customer focus, marketing skills, and open style made it the provider of choice. The clincher was that it was ready to start on the project immediately.

Another, more subtle factor that influenced Corning's choice of vendor was cultural fit. The core of Corning's deeply ingrained beliefs and behaviors are attributable to its long-term family ownership and hands-on operation and to the additional fact that, headquartered in rural upstate New York, the corporate culture is less subject to external influences than are firms in large metropolitan areas. CEOs from 1851 through 1995 were members of the caring, polite Houghton family. The behavior they modeled for generations is embedded in distinctive ways of interacting and conducting meetings. At Corning, it is more customary to hear statements like "I wonder if you've considered another alternative," or "Let me push back on that for just a minute" than it is to hear "You're wrong" or "That's a terrible idea." Having grown up in the Corning corporate community, CCFL already embraced these attitudes and behaviors, and spoke the company's language. In addition, they had the advantage of being extremely process oriented. This came naturally. When Corning embarked on its all-out cultural change effort to implement total quality, CCFL delivered the training. The fact that the supplier embraced what it taught, and applied the principles to its own organization, provided another key element of the fit between cultures.

That may explain why Corning was interested in this company, but why were they interested in working with Corning? At least one of the competing bidders thought the relationship would result in a fatal loss of autonomy. But for CCFL, the relationship meant a large market expansion, a steadier volume of customers, increased cash flow, national exposure, and acquisition of an educational process from one of the best internal training organizations in the country. In addition, they were equally comfortable with the match of organizational cultures; there was mutual respect and open, honest communication.

NEGOTIATING THE CONTRACT

Once the decision to partner was made, the next step was to develop a contract. From the outset, this was approached thoughtfully and carefully. It was also clear to all concerned that this relationship had to be built on trust. They knew that writing an extremely detailed contract would likely tangle their ability to be flexible. On the other hand, as quality practitioners, they were all keenly aware of the importance of articulating clear requirements.

Thus, as they began the partnership, both parties contracted carefully in order to protect the quality of service. Materials and instructors used by Corning were to be continued for a six-month period and then changed only after consultation. The vendor had the right to cancel courses based on enrollment, but only after a warning to Corning's staff. Course evaluations would be forwarded to Corning within two weeks. Other contract clauses dealt with proprietary information, copyrights, and liability situations. After putting a lot of thought into the contract, neither partner has ever needed to use it to get the other to take action. The contracting process (each contract is for a three-year period) enables and ensures unified thinking, operational guidelines, and formal milestones for updating the relationship. It is not meant to limit or control activity or to spell out every eventuality of service.

The funding for the relationship was as nontraditional as the contract. Corning gave its skills courses to CCFL. In return, they got a monopoly on the internal corporate market. All necessary funding for the vendor then had to be earned by selling services to this market. There was no service-level agreement or guarantee of revenue, although there was some assistance in start-up costs. In this specific situation, the absence of guarantees led the supplier to intensify its focus on the customer, so that contractual limitations became irrelevant.

This initial emphasis on living by the market has changed over the first decade of the partnership. As the relationship has become closer, and new skills and services have been developed by the supplier, a greater percentage of work has been shifted to contracts and project funding. Currently, administrative fees support about half of the outsourcing relationship.

THE EVOLVING RELATIONSHIP

Clearly, outsourcing did not remove the training function from Corning or even from its training organization. There is more to the story of integration. A project team of partnership staff members met monthly to review the transition activity. Very quickly, this became a kind of partnering and trust-building exercise. They built a management structure that educated the vendor's staff, demonstrated the quality of their work (and thereby bolstered the confidence and comfort level of Corning's training group), and encouraged joint decision making. The major emphasis was on building a positive relationship. In time, the supplier's staff became part of Corning's strategic planning of the training function, not only at the corporate center but also with the various business divisions.

A Corning manager was assigned responsibility for the overall outsourcing relationship. This was in addition to individual managers who were involved with course decision making. Corning has never backed off from the decision to have a partnership manager whose job description formally includes the management of the CCFL/Corning relationship. The people who have held this position have been selected carefully. They have a strategic view of training and learning within the company and a special skill at building the kind of relationship required by a partnership.

Before long, the new training role in regard to the core competencies of the corporation took most of the attention of Corning's internal staff. The importance of their role in creating a corporate culture cushioned the pain of giving up courses and activities that had been the life of the training and education organization. Nevertheless, the transition was especially difficult for logistics coordinators who enjoyed their role, particularly their contacts with workshop participants and external vendors. As it became apparent that this new role was valued far more highly, made a real difference in the workplace, and was something that no one else could do as effectively, the staff moved almost completely away from the old courses. Gradually, responsibility for the skills courses shifted almost totally to the supplier.

The mechanics of the transition were handled through phased implementation, a practice that has been used repeatedly as new projects have been undertaken. The partners decided to make the transfer of activity transparent. Initially, 64 courses were sent to CCFL/Corning. That number was soon increased to 125; the total catalog now contains more than 250 courses.

During the eight years following the formation of the partnership, the core of responsibilities was successively defined and redefined. Table 8.1 shows the shift in responsibilities between CCFL and Corning over the four stages of this partnership.

While table 8.1 shows the evolution of the relationship, it does not give a feel for the kind of change that actually took place. Change is almost always messy, and some of the challenges involved trying new things, figuring out that they did not work, and then altering the course of action. There were several stages too short to define. In one, a decentralization effort resulted in the

Table 8.1. Evolving Responsibilities

Stage	CCFL	Corning
Before partnering	Work with some business units; public workshops	Individual entrepreneurs
Initial partnership	Administration of skills courses	Development and delivery of core courses
Joint organization	Manage skills courses; administer core	Installation of systems; consulting
Human resources	Responsibility for all courses	Strategic leadership Initiation of new strategic efforts

vendor interacting with tiny pockets of training across the corporation. In another, they and a tiny central department (1.5 FTE) tried to maintain a strategic direction. They all lived through these months, and fortunately, a perceptive corporate leadership group dealt with them before damage was done.

TODAY'S SERVICES

Today, CCFL/Corning provides comprehensive learning services to Corning employees. The allocation of the broad scope of responsibilities is illustrated in table 8.2.

Table 8.2. Division of Services

CCFL/Corning	
Corning	**CCFL**
Development of corporate initiatives	Delivery of corporate initiatives
New technologies	Management of skills and functional training
Identification and dissemination of best practices	Credit or degree programs
Management of CCFL/Corning alliance	External workshops and development resources

Specifically, CCFL currently provides the following services as part of its relationship with Corning:

- *E&T Search.* Through this program, they provide Corning employees with easy telephone access to an electronic database of some 10,000 courses, workshops, and consultants providing expertise in a wide variety of areas, including competitive general courses and deep-niche specialties. This resource offers the benefit of having summaries of customer feedback and evaluations, so that Corning employees are neither spending time in extensive research nor buying an unknown.

- *Workshops.* They offer comprehensive workshop services that include selection of instructors, development, updating and procuring or producing materials, management of facilities and logistics, registration and billing, and evaluation.

- *Design and Development.* They design and develop courses and workshops appropriate to audiences, often in collaboration with Corning, but also independently, once the requirements are clarified.

- *Degrees and Tuition Reimbursement.* They offer a number of undergraduate and graduate degrees as well as certification programs. Services include management of Corning's tuition reimbursement upon successful completion of courses.

- *Sales to Other Companies.* Corning makes many of its training and education programs available to some of its customers and suppliers, as well as to subsidiaries and equity companies. CCFL is the agency that provides these services, tailoring them as needed to ensure a good fit with the culture of these external organizations.

EVALUATING TO ENSURE QUALITY

One of the important questions for the CCFL/Corning partnership to address has been how to ensure that a single source of supply maintains world-class quality performance in a noncompetitive situation. The design of the partnership includes several elements that address this issue. One essential process is maintaining regular reviews of the relationship. A supplier certification system, benchmarking, and above all, active management of the relationship have been helpful practices in the quality assurance effort.

At CCFL/Corning, continuous improvement also has been fueled by constant change in the relationship. New roles and responsibilities have forced the partners to evaluate and improve their old systems or to create new ones. The corporate management has not hesitated to demand lower costs, shorter time frames, and more results. These needs are not cushioned by the partnership—quite the opposite. To maintain their place in the corporate marketplace, the partners have had to address these issues directly. They have undergone evaluations by central corporate departments outside of education and training, including purchasing, quality, and control-treasury. The business divisions have the opportunity to do their own training if they believe that this would be more effective. In summary, the market-driven nature of the funding has kept the partners hungry and scared enough to ensure that they work hard at being the best supplier of their customers' training and education needs.

Another key question the partnership faced was how to evaluate their outsourced relationship. They developed success measures that tied back to the strategic plan—measures that pointed to the original motivations to outsource: flat budget; end-of-course evaluations; development of new courses; course cancellation rate; and manager, coordinator, and consultant evaluation. These measures did not focus on workshop effectiveness, however, and the decision to use them was criticized by some people who said that the focus should have been on increasing the impact of the workshops. But greater impact was not a goal when the relationship originated. Corning did not want a revolution in the approach; they wanted stability. It was not long, however, before training effectiveness did became a goal, and when it did, the partners addressed it. Current evaluation efforts are focused less on the relationship than on the learning and training it supports. Key tools are Corning's climate survey, key results indicators (KRIs), and selected, in-depth evaluations. End-of-course forms have not been abandoned, nor have instructor reviews.

THE WISDOM OF HINDSIGHT

Looking back from the perspective that only the passing of time allows, the partners can now see what worked well and what they would have done differently. The CCFL/Corning relationship has been successful and long lasting for a number of important reasons. The first of these is that Corning consistently put the right people in place to lead the effort. They had the appropriate blend of technical skill and the ability to nurture and manage a growing relationship. As the programs developed, partners focused on putting the right managers in charge of projects, an investment of time that has paid off handsomely.

Second, using a phased implementation plan was unquestionably a sound decision. The partners were able to pilot and improve processes and fix mistakes early in the game. As a result, they were never faced with huge, insurmountable problems or systems that were out of control. In fact, this approach has enabled them to achieve full implementation of programs faster than would have been possible with an all-at-once approach.

A third decision that led to success was the vendor's market focus—to find and delight customers. Although they enjoyed many advantages as the chosen supplier, they understood that as a privilege, not a right, and developed strategies aimed at encouraging Corning to choose them again and again.

Fourth, Corning's strategic emphasis proved to be wise for many reasons. By concentrating their internal resources on developing those critical competencies, they were able to shape the desired organizational change. In addition, because this job was so very important to the corporation, the training staff felt deeply valued at a time when they could have felt undermined, making for a smooth transition.

A fifth essential element in the success of this partnership was trust—trust based on an existing relationship and the result of well-matched organizational cultures, which made possible a kind of honesty that often seems risky. This trust has allowed both partners to share information that is often hidden, making it possible for them to work together in ways that have created mutual success.

Finally, the selective nature of the outsourcing relationship has provided many benefits, some of which were not anticipated at the beginning. The partners have had the opportunity to learn from each other and to grow. It has seemed to be the best of both worlds: an external supplier offering fresh perspective as well as a solid core of services, and a world-class company, often pioneering cutting-edge approaches to organizational change, as well as having the ability to resource projects appropriately.

As rewarding and beneficial as these elements have been, there are some experiences the partners have tried not to repeat. Finding and retaining qualified employees in a relatively small employment pool has sometimes been problematic. As a not-for-profit organization, CCFL's pay scale is not of the sort that makes it possible to recruit outside their geographic area. Yet success depends on careful, detailed oversight, managed by processes and to standards. Sometimes these jobs have been hard to fill. At other times, the supplier has invested in developing good people, only to have them leave. Turnover has been a problem as they have tried to ensure long-standing, close relationships with various customer groups.

Another aspect of the people-management issue has been the management of vendors. CCFL is able to be flexible and deliver a wide range of training products and services by utilizing a number of suppliers, from individual contracting instructors and course-development specialists to large training firms with expertise in various content areas. Some of these vendors have been outstanding; others have been disappointing. Over time, CCFL has tightened its investigative processes with new vendors and has maintained constant, ongoing monitoring and evaluation of existing suppliers. But there are still occasional surprises, and some of them are unhappy ones.

The final area that has provided some difficulty is the split that sometimes has occurred between content and logistics. On occasion, Corning has asked its partner to set up a course, find instructors, and handle materials without involving them in the course content. This has made it particularly difficult to select and manage the instructors. It also has been a problem for course coordinators, who felt outside the loop and had difficulty developing ownership in their areas of responsibility. Having lived through the inevitable tough times as well as some moments of delight and glory, however, the partners take pride in the relationship that has developed and in the accomplishments they have achieved together.

CONCLUSION

Looking back now, what has this partnership accomplished? Here is a short list of what they have done:

- produced an increase in training available to Corning employees
- added new training services for customers
- increased customer satisfaction with training, as measured by surveys
- reduced the time required for course design and delivery

- stabilized workshop and course fees
- decreased the training and education budget (initially flat, but becoming smaller)
- moved training costs from allocated overhead to user fees
- developed external marketing for Corning courses
- enabled Corning's training group to refocus its energies on core values, systems installation, and strategic leadership

The CCFL/Corning relationship has paid off for both organizations. It has been able to grow with the major changes at Corning, including the reorganization of top management and the spin-off of two new companies. Corning's requirement for quality training and education for its employees is being well met. As new roles have been defined and new needs recognized, the relationship has expanded to meet them. CCFL/Corning is growing in every sense of the word—and thriving. This is one outsourcing relationship that really works.

9

MEASURING VALUE IN THE OUTSOURCING RELATIONSHIP

9

OVERVIEW

It is popular to talk about outsourcing and the concept of value in business, but when most people think about outsourcing training, the *value* they expect to receive is lower costs. Although cost is an important part of what an outsourced training alliance can offer, it is only one part.

In 1996 Berlex Laboratories, Incorporated, a pharmaceutical firm, outsourced to CCFL (College Center of the Finger Lakes) all of the training management and most training development and delivery for its East Coast workforce—some 500 employees. The potential partners were very deliberate about the creation of this relationship, crafting a portfolio of products and services uniquely tailored to Berlex's needs.

This chapter will describe a three-stage model created to guide the development of the alliance and identify the value Berlex receives from it. It will argue that companies considering outsourcing should identify their own unique value drivers early in the process and put in place a process to measure and evaluate the outsourcing relationship on an ongoing basis. Finally it will show the process and specific tools in place at Berlex that provide feedback about the Berlex-CCFL alliance.

It is important to remember to evaluate not the outsourced training, per se, but the relationship with the outsourced partner that is providing the training functions. The model can be used as an ongoing review of the outsourcing relationship, not only to monitor but also to continually improve the relationship and services provided through the partnership. In addition, although many of the concepts apply equally to any company, the model described here is designed to be used by small- to medium-sized firms and does not include procedures for sampling very large employee populations.

ABOUT BERLEX

Berlex Laboratories, Incorporated, is the U.S. pharmaceutical affiliate of an international company founded in Germany more than 125 years ago. The company is committed to bringing to market beneficial preventive, diagnostic, and therapeutic medicines that address unmet medical needs. Berlex researches, manufactures, and markets ethical pharmaceuticals in three strategic areas: diagnostic imaging, female health care, and life-threatening and disabling diseases. The company employees approximately 1,400 people in its three divisions: Berlex Laboratories and Berlex Drug Development and Technology oversee the corporate and research administrative functions and are headquartered in New Jersey; Berlex Biosciences Division, which conducts basic research, is located in Richmond, California.

Berlex describes itself as "small enough for every employee to matter but large enough to have the resources necessary to get the job done." Its view is that its size prevents any employee from becoming a true specialist. Instead, Berlex has created a culture of growth. A commitment to ongoing employee development both through training and on-the-job challenges is linked to the company's strategy for growth.

LITERATURE REVIEW

There has been precious little written about how to evaluate the outsourcing relationship. Many of the current articles on outsourcing focus on the cost of outsourcing versus keeping functions in-house. Katherine Morall (1986) anecdotally discusses a study at the Savings Bank of Utica, New York, in which they compared the cost of outsourcing training with keeping it in-house (in this case, the Savings Bank of Utica found it more favorable to outsource training). Scott Lever (1997) explored how outsourcing is related to costs, risk, and satisfaction through sending out surveys to light manufacturing firms in the Northeast. And, consistent with other findings about the cost and value of outsourcing, John Dykeman (1996) cites a vice president of Kelly Management Services in Troy, Michigan, who claimed that a technical product manufacturer realized a 16 percent reduction in the cost of records management through outsourcing. None of these articles teaches the audience how to evaluate the outsourcing relationship once it has already been established.

Another main topic covered by current literature on outsourcing is how to start an outsourcing relationship. Margaret Kaeter (1995) discusses steps to consider prior to hiring an outsourced company. Garry DeRose and Janet McLaughlin (1995) also outline steps on how to decide whether or not to hire an outsourced partner. Both of these articles focus on the right questions to help establish the outsourced partnership; they do address the issue of how to establish value drivers for ongoing monitoring, improving, and optimizing the relationship once it has been established.

THE VALUE OF EVALUATING

Although many analyses of outsourcing have focused on cost, studies reveal that cost is not the biggest reason that companies outsource. One study (Williamson 1985) found that human resources (HR) executives are more likely to outsource when training is thought of as unique, idiosyncratic, or firm-specific, contrary to pure cost arguments. Similarly, the National Survey on Outsourcing Human Resource Services, conducted by Linkage, Incorporated, found that quality and flexibility, rather than cost, are "the most important variables in the outsourcing equation" (Harkins et al. 1995). Since cost is seldom the major driver in the decision to outsource, it is surprising to note that most review articles address only the costs saved. When setting up an evaluation scheme, it is important to consider some of the other value drivers in the decision to outsource.

There is another important reason to establish an evaluation process early on. In the study cited above, Lever noted that firms reporting higher levels of outsourced training also received more complaints about training. This problem can be prevented through monitoring and evaluating the quality of the services provided by the outsourced company *and* looking for ways to continually improve the service and relationship. Allowing the outsourced company to run unchecked, particularly if their service is poor, not only will hurt the outsourced group but also may damage the image of those managing outsourcing within the company. Ongoing evaluation can serve as a prevention method as well as a way to continue to optimize the relationship.

THE DECISION TO OUTSOURCE

At Berlex, the decision to outsource involved a lot more than just cost. The company established its first general training and organization development (OD) department in 1992, and by 1996, it had developed a fairly standard portfolio of training products and OD services. Three courses in a core curriculum focusing on building productive work relationships were developed and run for employees. The department also was researching and brokering other classes for specific needs, as well as fulfilling frequent individual requests for OD support. They discovered, however, that too much time and too much overhead were being devoted to maintaining the training program. The registration and reporting process was cumbersome and, because they were not experts in the local training market, they had to devote extensive research to each training request that could not be filled internally. The effort they invested on the front end getting the programs up and running prevented them from ensuring that their customers got top value from each program. In summary, although they had training activity, they did not have enough time to focus on the value in that activity.

At the same time, competitive pressures in the pharmaceutical industry were increasing dramatically. What was once a relatively stable industry had exploded with change as a result of sweeping national changes in health care. Berlex needed to respond by changing its own structures, systems, and processes, and it needed skilled training and development staff to work on these issues with internal customers in the line organizations. The internal staff was increasingly challenged to add more and more value for the company.

Berlex learned about CCFL at a conference in 1996 and immediately began discussions about how that organization might help leverage the time and skills of their internal staff. Rather than adopt a prepackaged approach, CCFL assessed the status of Berlex's programs and resources, and worked to create a customized solution. Their main challenges, which also became some of the value drivers for the alliance, were to accomplish the following tasks:

- handle all training logistics better than Berlex
- bring in new Berlex Basics skills development courses
- leverage the relationship with the Berlex frontline training and development staff
- provide more customized training for work groups
- free up the Berlex staff to think more strategically about development and the impact of all their activities

The model for evaluation of the alliance included specific areas of the alliance's *performance* as well as some of the subtler aspects of *value* described above. The core of the alliance involved managing the training infrastructure and included the following tasks:

- creation and distribution of two annual training calendars
- creation and distribution of monthly ad hoc marketing materials
- all training and conference registration, including courses offered externally
- establishment of 800 numbers and internal Berlex e-mail and voice mail access
- weekly, monthly, quarterly, and annual reporting
- all training logistics, including room reservations, food, audio-visuals, materials, and instructor logistics
- access to a database and search capabilities for individual training requests (called E&T Search)
- a preliminary needs assessment for new course possibilities

THE EVALUATION MODEL

The evaluation model came out of discussions about how to set up the relationship, and it reflected the value expected from the alliance. It is useful here to distinguish between managing the performance of an outsourced partner and evaluating the relationship. Typically, a contract to manage a vendor is written, and evaluation is the process used to determine how the vendor performs against the contract. Much of the current thinking about outsourcing emphasizes the importance of the relationship between the company and outsourced provider. Because these kinds of arrangements are not intended to be short term, it is important to find alignment between the goals and values of the partner organizations. Berlex was looking for a partner, not a vendor.

In any relationship, there are day-to-day issues that need to be negotiated and monitored. But with an outsourcing partnership, it is both possible and valuable to undertake a bigger-picture evaluation of the relationship. This is by definition subjective and uses the value drivers unique to each party. Because an outsourcing partnership is much more holistic than a traditional vendor-customer relationship, the evaluative process must consider more than just the sum of the parts of the relationship. Whereas performance management is based on the specific goals and objectives agreed to, the evaluation process is more subjective, longer term, two-way, and broader than the management of vendor performance.

The Berlex evaluation approach (see figure 9.1) provides a three-stage hierarchy to understanding and monitoring the outsourcing relationship. At its foundation is satisfaction with the products and services of the alliance, which has been created to provide specific services to the company. The starting point of any evaluation has to be here. It is hard to imagine any circumstance in which satisfaction with the core products and services could be low and yet the alliance would yield high value for both organizations.

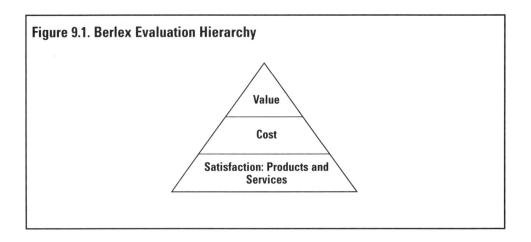

Figure 9.1. Berlex Evaluation Hierarchy

The second stage in the model is cost. Berlex wants high satisfaction with what the alliance produces, but it also wants those products and services delivered at a competitive cost. In this case *competitive* is evaluated relative both to other providers and to what it would cost to deliver the services internally. Finally, Berlex wants the alliance to deliver value to the company beyond good products, services, and competitive costs. This area is subjective and probably is unique for each organization, but it is critical for understanding the long-term impact of bringing the two organizations together.

In order to keep track of the measures, Berlex created a scorecard of these different dimensions, derived from Robert Kaplan and David Norton's (1992) "balanced scorecard" concept. The scorecard is designed to give top management fast access to a comprehensive view of the business by tracking a varied but balanced set of measures. Kaplan and Norton's model provides financial and operational measures, including customer satisfaction, internal processes, and organizational innovation. Berlex uses slightly different dimensions of measurement, but using multiple measures from different areas helps to ensure that the overall view of the relationship is balanced. Satisfaction with products and services is measured either two or four times per year, depending on which products and services are being evaluated. Cost and value are measured annually as part of an all-day alliance evaluation and planning meeting. The rest of this chapter will provide an examination of the process and specific measures Berlex and CCFL use to evaluate their alliance.

EVALUATING CUSTOMER SATISFACTION

The foundation of the Berlex evaluation is the satisfaction of internal customers with the products and services delivered by the alliance. Evaluating the customer satisfaction dimension includes two steps:

1. Interview or survey customers on their satisfaction with the various services provided by the outsourced group.

2. Hold periodic discussions between the primary contact group in the company (human resources development [HRD]), and the outsourced group on their mutual satisfaction with the working relationship.

Any company that chooses to adopt such a customer satisfaction evaluation model will need to customize the questions it asks, according to the nature of its particular relationship with the outsourcing partner.

In the first step, Berlex identified the two primary customers of the alliance: Berlex employees and managers who use CCFL's services; and the HRD staff, who serve as the primary contact persons for managing the vendor. Next, they identified which of the supplier's products and services to measure: management of training registration services and training materials; their E&T Search services, through which they can find virtually any class an employee needs from their nationwide database of courses; and their course customization service, in which they help tailor a class for a particular work group by doing a needs assessment and identifying the appropriate consultant or trainer for the class.

Finally, Berlex segmented the products and services the vendor provides by identifying the outcomes that were to be achieved within each area. For example, they determined that as a result of the course registration process, internal customers should be able to do the following:

- reach the vendor immediately
- receive confirmation e-mail reminders prior to their class
- find the vendor's advertising materials helpful and informative
- find registering for training to be a simple, easy process

The evaluation includes both closed and open-ended questions. Some are based on desired outcomes, such as "On a scale of 1–7, how would you rate the calendar and advertisement materials provided by CCFL?" Interviews about customer satisfaction always include the question, "Do you have any thoughts or comments about your experience with CCFL, positive or negative?" This question often provides the richest material and enables Berlex to get a more holistic idea of the overall value of their outsourcing relationship.

The numerical rating questions eventually go into the scorecard. The open-ended questions are not listed in the scorecard, but the data they generate eventually contribute to the overall report on the value of the alliance. Table 9.1 shows Berlex's scorecard for customer satisfaction with registration and materials. The customer satisfaction dimension of the evaluation also includes scorecards for questions on the E&T Search and on customized classes, which are not listed here (see Appendix 3 for the questions used).

Table 9.1. Customer Satisfaction Scorecard			
	April 1997	July 1997	December 1997
Percent that reached CCFL immediately		85%	100%
Percent that received confirmation e-mail reminder	91%	100%	100%
Rating of calendar and advertisement materials	5.8	5.83	5.8
Rating of overall satisfaction with registering for training	5.95	6.16	6.47

The purpose of the customer satisfaction interviews is to get a feel for how the customers are reacting to the outsourced company. To help make the management of the evaluation process easier for the human resource specialists, questionnaires are kept short. Berlex asks only six questions on registration and materials, seven questions on E&T Search, and five on customized classes.

In each of the evaluations, Berlex has interviewed or surveyed between 28 and 55 employees. They have experimented with two different survey techniques: phone interviews and written surveys. Interviewing yields richer data, since the interviewer is able to probe, using indirect interviewing techniques about the employee or manager's responses to the subjective questions. The evaluation results each quarter—a series of snapshots—have prompted timely improvements to optimize the relationship.

For example, in the April 1997 survey, customers gave a high rating to their overall satisfaction with E&T Search. At the next evaluation in July, the rating was significantly lower. Through the subjective responses, Berlex was able to learn more specific reasons for this lower rating. As it turned out, customers thought E&T Search was not timely enough and that some of the suggested classes were held in inconvenient locations. When brought to their attention, the supplier immediately revamped its processes. At the next evaluation in December, both partners were pleased to see an improved rating in response to this question.

Another major part of the customer service evaluation consists of regularly scheduled meetings between the partnership managers. In most firms, the HR department selects the outsourced training group and then serves as its primary contact and coordinator within the company. This is the case with Berlex. An important aspect of evaluating customer satisfaction is for the partners to evaluate the quality and efficiency of their working relationship.

As a part of the alliance evaluation process, Berlex adds another dimension: Their HRD staff examines *itself* and how it has worked with the vendor and also asks the supplier to evaluate the Berlex HRD staff. Thus the evaluative process provides a rounded perspective of not only how the partners work together but also how the key participants themselves perceive each organization. This model acknowledges that the behavior of the Berlex HRD staff influences the quality of services CCFL can provide. The multiple perspectives acquired in this way make it possible to make adjustments that improve the alliance.

The topics for this subjective assessment process at Berlex are built on Valarie Zeithaml's (1990) model for understanding and evaluating service. He and his coauthors suggest that any service interaction, whether it is cashing a check at a bank or receiving training services, can be characterized by the variables of reliability, responsiveness, tangibles, empathy, and assurance. These variables are incorporated in a candid "How's it going?" conversation between the alliance partners approximately twice a year. For example, in these meetings the partners formally consider the turnaround time of each of the organizations: How long does it take each side to respond to requests from the other? They also review the quality of the written products, courses, and instructors. All members of both teams are present at each of these evaluations.

EVALUATING COST AND EFFICIENCY

The Berlex model for evaluating the cost and efficiency of the outsourced group includes two parts. The first evaluates the cost effectiveness of using an outsourced company versus keeping the training in-house. The second assesses the competitiveness of the current outsourced group versus other outsourced groups. It is important to evaluate cost and efficiency on an annual basis.

Cost of Outsourcing vs. Keeping Training In-house

The comparison of the cost of outsourcing versus keeping all the training functions in-house can be achieved by first listing the outputs, or the outcomes, that the outsourced company is to achieve. The next step is for the company to examine what it would cost to have permanent or temporary employees in-house to achieve those same outcomes. It is critical that real, or fully loaded, costs be used to achieve an honest comparison. The Berlex model incorporates all the costs of employment, including benefits and overhead for the people hired in-house. The cost of managing these employees is also included in the model.

The cost-efficiency aspect of the evaluation begins by listing the outputs, or deliverables, from the outsourced company, separating each task into the components that would normally be assigned to administrators versus those typically assigned to managers, as seen in table 9.2 (taken from the Berlex-CCFL contract).

Berlex created several models for how they might deliver those services internally. Since they had done this work themselves prior to the CCFL contract, however, they were fairly certain that to provide the services listed in table 9.2, they would need one full-time administrative employee and one-third of a training and development manager's time. They assumed that the cost of managing the manager up the hierarchy would be equivalent to the cost of managing the vendor. Thus they began by calculating the salary-and-benefits costs for one administrative employee and one-third of a manager.

Table 9.2. Training Alliance Outputs	
Administrative	**Managerial**
• Development and production of two training calendars per year, plus monthly advertising reminders • Phone, e-mail, and fax access eight hours per day to process registrations, confirmations, and requests for information • Production and distribution of all prework and classroom training materials • Preparation for training delivery: confirming rooms, notifying security, ordering food, ordering room setup, arranging for materials to be shipped to students, and preparing instructors • Specific classes for individual employees via E&T Search • Reporting: registration, utilization, and training satisfaction reports • All instructor and vendor billing • Management of internal chargebacks	• Management of customized training requests: assessing needs, creating project plans, choosing instructors and times, and arranging for the class to be implemented • Development and delivery of some internal courses • Overall training oversight: utilizing reporting information, determining training direction, managing internal stakeholders • Management of the administrative employee

Next, they assessed the fixed costs for these employees by using figures from actual department expenditures as well as estimates from the HR and finance departments and local real estate agents. They included projections for telephone, office space rental, facility allocation (lights, water, parking space), information technology hardware and software, hardware depreciation, computer support, training and development of the employees, travel expenses, and office supplies.

There was one aspect of the contract that Berlex could not provide within the above structure, however. The E&T Search service offered by CCFL involves access to proprietary training-and-development databases and considerable skill and experience at researching courses for specific individual requests. Berlex has a library and skilled librarians and imagined that one of these employees could conduct similar searches for courses and other training and OD resources. By estimating the number of general inquiries, the number of completed requests, and the amount of time required to process each, Berlex concluded that the effort would take 290 hours, or about 16.6

percent of a librarian's time. They then calculated the total value at the fully loaded cost for salary and benefits. Table 9.3 summarizes the cost structure at Berlex compared with the fixed contract cost from the vendor for the first year of operation.

Table 9.3. Comparison of Costs for E&T Search		
	CCFL	Berlex
Salaries		$ 70,736
Employment costs (benefits)		30,282
Overhead		22,013
Electronic search costs		16,972
Total Costs for Administration	$ 75,000	$ 140,003

During the first year of the contract, CCFL charged a flat fee of $75,000 for all of the services listed in table 9.2. Berlex made assumptions about volume and included provisions in the contract to increase the vendor's fee if volume was higher than expected. But because of its lower cost structure and greater internal efficiencies, CCFL's E&T Search was much more cost-effective than providing similar services in-house.

Estimating Competitiveness of Current Outsourcing Supplier

Occasionally it is valuable to consider the competitiveness of the out-sourced company by evaluating the cost of other similar outsourcing services. Cost is only one aspect of the larger value equation that companies should consider, but comparing an external reference point to the service used keeps both sides current with the market. Early in the contracting phase, Berlex talked with other vendors and received significantly higher cost estimates for roughly the same services. Thus they were satisfied that CCFL's combination of products, services, and approach was highly competitive.

EVALUATING VALUE

In his 1996 talk "Creating Value: New Models of Delivery for Staff Service" at the 1996 Strategic Outsourcing and HR Conference, David Ulrich defined *value* as *cost* × *quality.* Ulrich noted that value is defined by the receiver. At the same conference in an address entitled "Strategic HR Management: An Idea Whose Time Has Come," Edward Lawler said that value is a mix of speed, innovation, quality, and cost. Value, according to Lawler, creates effectiveness. In Berlex's view, value, in relation to outsourcing, is a holistic way of viewing the benefits a company receives from an outsourcing alliance *over and above cost, efficiency, and satisfaction.* Value refers to the overall impact or effect. In this interpretation, value cannot be completely understood transactionally or even quantitatively.

Although vendor performance can be quantified and measured, and is a key part of assessing the value of the relationship, value also involves enabling or increasing capabilities. Such amorphous factors are much more difficult to measure. Value in certain areas may not be identified or planned for in advance, yet it is critical for the long-term success of a relationship. Where a company looks for value will depend on its initial motivations for outsourcing, but where it finds it could be in broader areas than initially anticipated.

Berlex assesses the value of the outsourcing relationship informally on an ongoing basis, as well as formally once a year in an annual alliance meeting. While compiling information—from interviews on the topic of customer satisfaction, or in the yearly discussions about the alliance relationship, or in the evaluation of cost-efficiency—the evaluator may find stories or examples that demonstrate benefits from the alliance that are over and above the cost, efficiency, and satisfaction.

Berlex anticipated some aspects of value in two of the major drivers for their decision to outsource: (1) to enable the internal HRD staff to focus more on organization development and maximize their own value to the company; and (2) to bring higher capability to the training function. During the first year of the alliance, they were able to document the contributions the vendor made in these areas and others, beyond the provision of the contracted services.

Changes at Berlex That Demonstrate Value

First and foremost, the HRD staff noted a dramatic shift in what they needed to—and were able to—focus on. Whereas in the past, they had spent considerable time in the design and development of training programs and the coordination of logistics (registrations, room and materials preparation, reporting), now the staff could work with the executives on determining what type of training and development activities would best support their unit strategies, who should attend, and how the training would be followed up and measured. Instead of trying to create reports, the HRD staff was able to concentrate on how to use them. In short, the focus shifted from trying to create learning technologies to implementing and maximizing learning technologies. This created a significant jump in value to the customer business units.

There also were enabling gains that Berlex did not anticipate. In addition to registering employees for Berlex classes, as part of its base contract the vendor handles registration for outside classes and conferences. A Berlex secretary who is responsible for registering her departmental staff for training programs and conferences now needs to make only one call to the supplier. She described an involved process of researching programs, calling back and forth, and experiencing considerable aggravation before the alliance. Because all of this is now reduced to a single phone call, she is now able to perform more value-adding tasks in the department, an unanticipated, positive benefit.

In addition, prior to partnering with CCFL, Berlex managed a complex system of internal and external billing as an outcome of the training process. External vendors billed the Accounts Payable Department for courses. The follow-up internal audit and chargeback system required considerable HR staff time to verify and adjust bills, and to input information about employee cost centers. CCFL has assumed all billing responsibilities for all vendors and submits one comprehensive bill each month, which includes all chargeback and verification data. No additional input of information is needed, saving considerable time and effort.

Capability Outcomes That Demonstrate Value

In addition to considering how certain outcomes confer value, it is also possible to look at how some particular capabilities provide value. Although Berlex employs qualified training and development staff, their partner's *only* business is training and development. Because this is their sole focus and because they provide these services for many different companies, they have some capabilities that a company like Berlex does not have—and probably should not have. For example, they stay abreast of cutting-edge learning technologies, and when new training needs come up at Berlex, they make recommendations about the most effective methods for addressing them.

The vendor has numerous resources that can be put to use in the service of its clients, drawing on an internal staff of instructional designers, platform trainers, and production specialists that Berlex does not have. They design, develop, and deliver their own training and maintain a wide network of trainers and programs they can broker to Berlex when needed for specific training needs. E&T Search provides another capability that is of great value to Berlex. In the past when individual managers or employees requested specialized training courses, Berlex had to research each one from scratch. Not having special databases or extensive search knowledge meant these requests could be very time consuming and frustrating for both the requestor and the HRD staff. Now their partner has all of these capabilities in place and returns a customized report listing a variety of classes that meet the requestor's criteria within two weeks of the date of request.

Finally, CCFL adds value to the alliance by providing centralized data about total companywide training utilization. This enables the Berlex HRD staff to work more effectively with their customers about how to plan for and utilize training opportunities. Interestingly, some of the most useful information concerns who *did not* attend training or who canceled. This data also provides better information about which programs to offer by tracking enrollments, interest, and feedback on classes.

CONCLUSION

Berlex finds real benefit from its outsourcing alliance. What gives them confidence, however, is not just that everyone feels good about the partnership, but that the measurements demonstrate its worth. When Berlex initially explored and then established the alliance, they tried to be clear about what they were seeking to achieve. An important part of that process was to deliberately establish not only some quantifiable measures of success but also the less tangible ones. By establishing a methodology and process for testing outcomes on a regular basis, they have acquired the most useful of all tools for continuous improvement—information.

The basic principles of measurement presented in this chapter, coupled with practical examples and tools revealing how they are applied at Berlex, provide a value-based model for measuring the outsourcing of training and education. Others who are exploring the opportunities that outsourcing affords are invited to borrow from Berlex's experiences as they implement programs that add value to their companies.

References

DeRose, Garry, and Janet McLaughlin. (1995, October). "Outsourcing Through Partnerships." *Training and Development,* 51–55.

Dykeman, John. (1996). "Should You Farm Out Records Management?" *Managing Office Technology, 41* (7), 34–36.

Harkins, Philip J., Stephen M. Brown, and Russel Sullivan. (1995, December). "Shining New Light on a Growing Trend." *HRMagazine,* 75–79.

Kaeter, Margaret. (1995, November). "An Outsourcing Primer." *Training and Development,* 20–26.

Kaplan, Robert S., and David P. Norton. (1992, January-February). "The Balanced Scorecard: Measures That Drive Performance." *Harvard Business Review,* 71–79.

Lawler, Edward III. (1996). "Strategic HR Management: An Idea Whose Time Has Come." In *The International Conference and Exposition on Strategic Outsourcing and HR: Leveraging the Business Impact of Human Resources.* New Orleans: Linkage Incorporated and The George Washington University.

Lever, Scott. (1997). "An Analysis of Managerial Motivations Behind Outsourcing Practices in Human Resources." *Human Resources Planning, 20* (2), 37–61.

Morall, Katherine. (1986). "Bringing Training In-house Without the In-house Costs." *Bank Marketing,* (28), 43–47.

Ulrich, David. (1996). "Creating Value: New Models of Delivery for Staff Services." In *The International Conference and Exposition on Strategic Outsourcing and HR: Leveraging the Business Impact of Human Resources.* New Orleans: Linkage Incorporated and The George Washington University.

Williamson, Oliver E. (1985). *Economic Institutions of Capitalism.* New York: The Free Press. Quoted in Scott Lever, (1997). "An Analysis of Managerial Motivations Behind Outsourcing Practices in Human Resources." *Human Resources Planning, 20* (2), 37–61.

Zeithaml, Valarie A., A. Parasuraman, and Leonard L. Berry. (1990). *Delivering Quality Service: Balancing Customer Perceptions and Expectations.* New York: The Free Press.

About the Contributors

James Shillaber is the director of organization effectiveness and training at Berlex Laboratories, a New Jersey-based pharmaceutical company. In this role, he brings people-development systems and technologies to key business problems. His department delivers frontline human resources services and provides consultation, organization development, and training for Berlex's

East Coast employees. Prior to joining Berlex, James was an external consultant, helping telecommunications, financial and pharmaceutical companies align their structures, systems, culture, and people with business strategy. He is a clinical psychologist and family therapist.

Alexandra P. Miller worked on this chapter while serving an internship at Berlex. She is currently working toward a doctorate in organizational psychology at Rutgers University's Graduate School of Applied and Professional Psychology. She received her B.A. degree in public policy studies from Duke University.

10

LEARNING FROM EXPERIENCE

10

This book has attempted to present an overview of the opportunities for learning gleaned from the experience of many practitioners in the outsourcing field. The final chapter is organized into four sections that categorize some of the major learning topics:

- Success Factors
- Special Attention
- Kiss of Death
- The Final Word: System

SUCCESS FACTORS

The outsourcing partnerships that have survived for several years—or at least those that are off to a good start—have a number of factors in common. These factors, which will be explored briefly with elucidation from some pertinent examples, are as follows:

- Match the model to the need.
- Change will happen; flexibility is essential.
- Build and adjust; implement in phases.
- The company's agenda reigns.
- Manage the partnership.
- Both partners are 100 percent responsible for success.
- Focus on strategic goals, not just dollars saved.

Overarching all of these elements is a thoughtfully planned process such as the one outlined in chapter 2. Only by developing and agreeing upon such a process can the partners ensure that their own needs are addressed, establish an appropriate understanding of prospective partners' needs and capabilities, and lay the groundwork for a successful working relationship. All of the elements listed here can be designed into both prospective partners' processes for exploring, planning, and implementing an outsourcing project. It would undoubtedly benefit those who are considering or planning such a venture to review their plans and ensure that they have built in these factors.

Match the Model to the Need

The five case studies presented in chapters 4 through 8 reveal several different outsourcing models. The reason that all of them are now working is that each has developed a model that matches the particular needs of the company with the capabilities of its partners. While it is undoubtedly valuable to explore the differences among these and, for those who are considering an outsourcing project, to identify the one that most closely matches their own organization's requirements, it would be unfortunate to stop there. Elements may be borrowed from these and other models and examples, but in the end, each outsourcing arrangement must respect the uniqueness of the organizations involved and, accordingly, must be designed to fit them exactly.

The benefits of benchmarking others' experiences are evident in the cases of Dow, Corning, and Quest. All of these companies formed partnerships based on a single-partner model. The relationships have strengthened and grown over time. Essentially, each began by using the partner to provide the logistics of training delivery. Dow has kept that arrangement fundamentally the same throughout its relationship with Delta. Corning has asked CCFL to take on more and more responsibilities, but logistics remain at the center of what they provide. Quest began with the intention of using CCFL for logistics, but quickly decided to turn over course design and development, as well as logistics. What emerged was essentially a single-source comprehensive model for outsourcing of training and development.

Like these companies, Kaiser Permanente began its outsourcing process with a single-partner, logistics model. The staff quickly learned that this would not work for them, however, and to their credit, undertook to change the model very quickly. The sheer size of their organization, the geographic distribution of their sites, the special needs for technical training, and the accurate tracking of that training all placed special demands on their outsourcing situation. As it turned out, no single supplier had sufficient diversity of expertise to handle these multiple and complex needs. Thus they wound up building a complex, multipartner model that now appears to be much better suited to their situation.

In addition to such factors as size and complexity, the particular organizational goals and purpose for outsourcing also influence the selection and development of the outsourcing model. Because Corning's primary goal was to focus on strategic initiatives, it made sense for them to utilize a single supplier with not only logistical capabilities but also the capacity to provide design and development that is responsive to their strategic intent. Beyond these broad differences, each partnership must develop its own style of doing business together that becomes part of its model. For example, the CCFL/Corning partnership operates with a contract that provides general guidelines but deliberately avoids a listing of detailed requirements.

What all of this adds up to is the need for organizations to be fairly introspective, define their own needs clearly, and begin with a model that borrows appropriately from others, but primarily meets the current needs and anticipates future ones. This lays the groundwork for the partners to grow the model, along with their relationship, together over time. While a simple, clean model is certainly desirable, the experiences of these companies and others have demonstrated that the path to choosing the most suitable design usually contains many curves, and sometimes a detour or two.

Change Will Happen

In every outsourcing partnership discussed in this book, its planners discovered that what they thought they wanted was not what they got. This is not to suggest that their planning was pointless—quite the contrary. The more concrete information a company can utilize to understand its current requirements and project its future needs, the better the foundation that can be laid for the inevitable changes.

Virtually everyone in this business has discovered that it is nearly impossible to anticipate the next three to five years following the inception of an outsourcing partnership. In part, changes that affect the partnership are generated by changes in the business: new initiatives, changes in the industry or marketplace in which they play, and changes in personnel elsewhere in the company. In addition, of course, changes occur as internal customers make new discoveries about their training and development needs when they realize what is potentially available to them. Thus outsourcing partnerships must build in the capability to be flexible.

There is another experience common among those who have undertaken the outsourcing process that is uncommon in most other business relationships. This one contains some elements of mystery. In nearly every long-term outsourcing effort, a moment occurs when the planners quite suddenly discover some critical factors not previously considered. This happens despite the best efforts of intelligent, thoughtful, analytic planners. It has the quality of a revelation, though a very uncomfortable one. And it inevitably brings the process to an abrupt and complete halt. Following this epiphany, the planners reassess the situation and adjust accordingly. Thus flexibility is required to adjust not only for the predicted changes and the unpredictable-but-anticipated changes but also for these rather startling manifestations of truth.

Examples of metamorphoses abound. The CCFL/Corning partnership of 1998 would be recognizable only in its broadest structure to those who started it in 1987. Business changes have led to at least five different versions of this partnership. Environmental shifts have included changes in upper management, companywide reengineering, the spin-off of two new companies and the sale of a major division, the evolution of an ever-more-sophisticated human resources strategy, and enormous changes in many of the marketplaces in which this high-tech company plays. In addition, of course, there have been some changes in the personnel responsible for training and development, and in the management of the partnership. In broad terms, CCFL/Corning has gone from a partnership based on the outsourcing of skills, to one in which virtually all aspects of training were outsourced, to the current hybrid of skills-based and strategic endeavors. For now, the operation is stable. But the partners understand that like many organizations, the partnership is organic; it will change.

The Quest Diagnostics–CCFL partnership is much newer and, therefore, has undergone fewer changes. But the shift that has occurred has been very dramatic. Quest began by requesting traditional training—perhaps a version of the Corning outsourcing experience in its early stage. They were so sure of the merits of that approach, they developed a detailed contract to handle precisely that situation. What they discovered was that almost 100 percent of the work being outsourced was in service to strategic initiatives. Quest made the decision to focus their internal staff on strategy development, and turned over virtually all the training and development activities in support of these to the vendor. Once again, flexibility was essential.

The Dow-Delta case study reveals that they too underwent some dramatic changes in the structure of their partnership. There was a natural evolution toward Delta's assumption of more and more responsibilities. More recently, reengineering at Dow has led to a significant change in the company's human resource development structure. These changes have led in turn to newly defined competencies and a whole new set of training requirements for Delta to implement simultaneously worldwide. On its side, Delta too underwent restructuring and growth. Its increased capabilities and improved systems meant that Dow could make better use of its partner's capabilities.

Perhaps the most dramatic changes in partnership were those of Kaiser Permanente (KP). After many months of investigation and planning, KP terminated its first partnership less than three months after it started, devised a whole new multipartner model, and had significant pieces of that up and running within a very few months.

The lesson from all of these experiences is that partners can depend on change occurring. At times, it will occur slowly, in an orderly, evolutionary way. At others, it will occur in a blinding burst of energy. An example of the latter is the crisis that occurs in about the third year of any partnership. Unplanned and unforeseen, this event has the effect of recentering the partnership. There even seems to be a rationale for this. Typically, the partnership has jelled. The work that they do can no longer be described as being in the start-up phase. They begin to have a body of actual data that brings sometimes-harsh reality to the initial euphoria. Tough questions get asked. Both partners take a hard look at the payoffs for this arrangement. And, too, simply because many companies need to ensure that their employees remain challenged, changes in partnership personnel often occur simultaneously. The result: a crisis—often full blown, and potentially destructive.

In the face of such a situation, and others less severe, partners are most likely to succeed if they take a fresh look at the situation, with an openness to examining what it is now and what has changed. Trying to make the current situation fit the original model results in confusion, frustration, and most probably the wrong next steps. Successful partnership managers seem to take an objective, historical view. They try to detect new patterns and alter the model and the partnership to suit them. This is where a contractual framework rather than a contractual straitjacket becomes a real advantage. Or, if a detailed contract was originally written, it should at least include an escape clause that enables the partners to abandon Plan A and move to Plan B. *Flexibility* may seem like a modest word for such circumstances. But whatever the size and shape of change, outsourcing partners—and particularly the suppliers—seem to fare best when they are pliant and elastic, without losing the essence of who they are and what they do best.

Build and Adjust

There is one strategy, however, that can help partners to plan for and adjust to the changes they create together. This is to build opportunities for learning and adjustment into the implementation of any project. The decision diamond model outlined in chapter 2 provides a formalized structure for this, which can be applied at just about any stage of a project's development. In some situations where the start-up has ranged from rocky to disastrous, one factor that appears to be missing in every case is a phased implementation plan with decision diamonds built in to learn from the past and adjust for the future. Certainly such points will frequently yield some surprises, but even the exercise of anticipating them together sometimes enables partners to refine their plan even before it is first launched.

Building a plan of phased implementation from the outset positively affects the success of the project over the long term. Start with a very small portion of the projected task and build in very deliberate checkpoints for gathering information; then assess and adjust before beginning a larger-scale implementation. After this first round of transfer and learning, the rest of the implementation schedule can be divided into phases that incorporate decision diamonds. Although the early decision diamonds are most productive in helping to lay the groundwork for working together, the checkpoints that occur later in the project will help identify changes and facilitate adjustments before they became full-blown crises.

Although many factors contributed to the early difficulties Kaiser Permanente experienced, including the complexity of KP's needs when matched with the less comprehensive capabilities of its partner, the outcome might have been different if more time had been built into their implementation plan. The three-month crunch of activity simply did not allow time for learning and adjustment. Even planning for decision diamonds collaboratively might have led both partners into a clearer discussion of expectations and capabilities before the project was launched. While no 20/20 hindsight can undo the past and provide absolute answers, there is some value in exploring what might have made a difference.

The Company's Agenda Reigns

Another factor that clearly affects the success of an outsourcing partnership is a very clear focus on the company's agenda and needs. While this variation on the maxim "The customer is always right" may seem obvious, it is violated with amazing frequency in numerous business situations. Certainly it is a principle that must not be ignored in a relationship as deep and close as the outsourcing partnership needs to be.

The goal in outsourcing is always for the service provider to meet its partner's needs. Sometimes this can mean helping the company to discover things about its present or future that it has not recognized on its own. Such a skill can yield opportunities for both partners to grow. Nevertheless, if this process is subverted—even unconsciously—to focus on the wishes of the provider rather than the company, then the outsourcing relationship is doomed. Most of the disasters reviewed in this book have involved a vendor with a portfolio of products and services to sell or another compelling interest that takes precedence over a genuine, dispassionate focus on its partner's needs. This is not to say that providers with a special body of expertise or an interest in benefiting their own organization cannot be highly successful partners. Certainly all providers are in business for some gain. The real question is one of focus: Any time it becomes too clouded by self-interest, there is trouble in the making.

In general terms, companies should be extremely cautious about considering a partnership with a "specialty" provider. Even though some very sophisticated organizations can offer high levels of knowledge, they also have built-in biases. For example, to a company that specializes in organizational development, all of their customers' problems and issues begin to look solvable by organizational development interventions. This is not necessarily subversive. It is simply what they are deeply immersed in, what they know extremely well, and what they probably have great skill in applying. Organizational development, however, is not necessarily the only or even the best approach for solving all of a company's training, education, and development needs. Thus such a provider may be a superb consultant but a potentially disastrous outsourcing partner. The reason: Their focus is too much influenced by their own expertise and too little by a clear-sighted, unbiased understanding of the company's needs.

This issue is illustrated in Compaq's first partnership with PDI, one of their valued suppliers whose base of expertise is in management development. Compaq and PDI enjoyed an excellent relationship as customer and vendor, and fortunately, do so once again. But their foray into an outsourcing partnership nearly spelled disaster for their relationship. While PDI was (and is) highly skilled at design, delivery, and assessment of programs to improve leadership, the move into coordinating training and orientation, marketing courses, and administration of tuition assistance took them on a serious detour from their mission. With complete integrity, they intended to meet their partner's needs, but their whole organizational culture made it virtually impossible for them to do so effectively.

A more extreme example of how a supplier's focus on the wrong things can hurt a relationship is that of a college that entered the outsourcing arena. This not-for-profit institution saw a partnership with a large company as a way to justify capital expenditures for a greatly desired auditorium. While it is certainly possible that such a building program might be helped by a business-college partnership, the problem arose because the building was the college's real, although hidden, focus. Thus, instead of seeking to understand the company's requirements, they did the reverse: They completely ignored them. As a result, the college built a structure that lacked sufficient telephones, restrooms, and other essential facilities required for corporate training purposes.

As with the other lessons learned, the issue here is not one of absolutes but of degree and nuance. Any prospective supplier that claims not to be interested in fulfilling its own mission probably ought not to be in business. And any company that insists on its own way all the time and is entirely inflexible is probably an impossible customer. If the vendor does not push back on a company and offer its unbiased wisdom, it is not providing a good service. For a supplier to let self-interest color a genuine understanding of its partner's needs beyond the palest tints, however, can only spell disaster.

The final two success factors have already been addressed in chapter 2. Nevertheless, they are worth touching on again briefly here because they are so essential to the success of an outsourcing project.

Manage the Partnership

Managing an outsourcing partnership is by no means an impossible job, but any attempt to write a detailed job description will make it seem so.

Successful partnership managers have in common many of the same strengths as other good managers. Among these are strong project management skills and people skills. One of the differences, however, is that while these strengths may be sufficient to excel in certain types of line-management jobs, they are not, by themselves, enough for partnership managers. Some additional strengths are required.

One significant add-on seems to be the ability to mediate, negotiate, and persuade, as opposed to issuing directives. Partnership managers must frequently operate from a base of personal power rather than linear power, and their ability to leverage that can make or break a project. On the basis of their own capabilities rather than the weight of their positions, they can accomplish some remarkable things—bring about 180-degree shifts in philosophy, shake loose "impossible" funding, buy time to re-create the entire project.

A second add-on is the ability to work with some ambiguity, finding patterns and order within experiences, particularly as change occurs. This means being comfortable with some unknowns, developing the ability to extract knowledge from scattered and sometimes entirely new sources of information, and the ability to inspire confidence in others while things are in a state of flux. As case after case has revealed, outsourcing always involves change. Successful outsourcing managers have some understanding of what this means and sufficient comfort with it to allow them to remain sane when others might implode. They search for meaning, on an intuitive level as well as in a deliberate plan, and translate what they learn to others.

From the supplier's perspective, it is important to take note of how the company's partnership manager operates—to pay attention to the human factors, particularly those of the leaders. Developing an understanding of their personal managerial styles makes it possible to anticipate needs and provide a better service. Understanding what human skills and factors affect the success of the partnership provides information to share as transitions in personnel occur. This is important, after all, because companies make a big investment in developing outsourcing relationships, and maintaining them as smoothly as possible through changes in the cast of characters is a business issue.

Both Are Responsible for Success

This, too, is a human issue. While it is easy to say on paper that both sides accept responsibility for the success of the outsourcing venture, success happens because people make it happen. Managers and staff members in whom that concept is deeply embedded reflect the concept of total responsibility in their values and behavior.

This attitude is linked to total quality. An emphasis on quality has produced some remarkable differences among the organizations that have applied it. Several helpful attitudes emerge. There is a conscious effort not to lay blame. Problems are addressed as learning opportunities. Candid discussions about what went right and what went wrong are a way of doing business. Even when there is a crisis, the approach to solving it is grounded in a seemingly simple but profound principle: Each partner is 100 percent responsible for success.

Focus on Strategic Goals

If a company's goal is to reduce training costs, then the easiest solution is to reduce training. To make cost reduction the primary goal of outsourcing is to hang a dark cloud directly above the venture from its inception. It focuses everyone's attention on the wrong goals, with predictable results.

A more appropriate goal of outsourcing is framed in a question such as this: How can this company best develop employee, organizational, and company-wide skills in a cost-effective and cost-efficient manner? The question of how much an outsourcing partnership can trim from the cost of an internal operation is very difficult to measure, since they are not run in parallel, at the same point in time. But the flexibility of a supplier's staffing certainly provides the opportunity to yield some savings. In CCFL's experience, the average cost saving of a successful outsourcing is roughly 30 percent.

In such a context, cost reduction can be a delightful side effect of the outsourcing process. There are other means to achieve this end, however. Although outsourcing can yield quick, major financial results, the fact is that most of these are achieved when the internal operation has been inefficiently managed. Opportunities for improved efficiency and effectiveness, with concomitant fiscal gains, are uncovered in almost every company that considers outsourcing. A thorough audit of its existing training organizations frequently reveals not only redundant courses but also redundant training departments within the same company. Unfavorable cancellation policies or sloppy enforcement of sound policies are other common reasons for loss. Sometimes it is to a company's advantage to bring in an outsourcing partner to clean up such situations. But often the benefits of such a service are outweighed by the cost of the transfer to the outsourcing partner. Ideally, improvement initiatives should be undertaken before the outsourcing partnership is initiated. In this way, both partners have a realistic basis on which to measure the benefits and costs of outsourcing.

The erroneous goal of cost reduction deserves special consideration because it is so frequently mentioned (or thinly disguised) as the major reason to outsource. In fact, successful outsourcing is much like a successful internal operation. It focuses on achieving the company's strategic goals, assesses the company's present and future needs, develops a plan for developing employees' capabilities to align with these, and creates effective learning systems to deliver them.

Outsourcing is simply one tool for accomplishing these organizational goals. A growing number of successful outsourcing partnerships demonstrate that it can be a very good tool. External partners can bring deep-niche expertise, fresh perspectives, additional services, and other benefits in their portfolio of services. They are, or should be, experts in the matter of learning and development. That is their core competency. And whether a customer employs 40 people or 40,000, there can be a real advantage in partnering with such an expert. But only if the customer stays focused on its own strategic intent.

The factors outlined in this section—the model or need, flexibility, phased implementation, company focus, partnership management, mutual complete responsibility, and appropriate goals—have proved again and again to have a profound impact on the success of outsourcing. Doing them well goes a long way toward making the ventures succeed. Doing them poorly hurts immeasurably.

SPECIAL ATTENTION

There are some other matters, however, that deserve special attention largely because they have proved difficult to do well. These are not issues that have hit the headlines as guaranteeing success or heralding failure. Nonetheless, the following actions are very real and important to both partners and worth the investment of time and energy to learn to do successfully:

- Create a mutually beneficial fee structure.
- Develop a training strategy.
- Handle internal staff well.

- Communicate forcefully with suppliers.
- Build and maintain trust.

Create a Mutually Beneficial Fee Structure

The obvious point is this: Companies want to save money; vendors want to earn money. The tough question is how to balance these needs. How can planners make the arrangement profitable for both parties, and how can they accomplish this in a way that both partners feel assured of its fairness? How does the agreement preserve the partnership through bad times as well as good? How does the company ensure that its partner remain market focused over the long term? How do partners deal with new projects, changes, and flux in volume?

These questions are addressed in various ways. Companies that engage in outsourcing commonly use four different approaches, which are outlined briefly below. Each, of course, is subject to variation and permutation.

Flat Fee

In a flat-fee agreement, a company consents to pay a fixed sum for a defined group of services. The advantage of such an arrangement for the company is that it eliminates the unhappy possibility of cost overruns. The advantage to the supplier is that it provides a known amount of revenue, which it can presumably manage to ensure at least a modest profit.

The major drawbacks of such an arrangement are that it builds in no incentive for performance excellence, and that it does not accommodate shifts in volume or type of service provided. These can certainly be pitfalls for the customer, in that it is quite possible to get a much smaller or lower level of service than had been expected. Conversely, the supplier must be cautious about "scope creep" in which the demand for service rises in ways that may be so small individually as to be almost unnoticeable, but can cumulatively add up to a sizable incremental difference.

A candid discussion and clear statement of both their quantitative and qualitative expectations can help partners to avoid some of these problems. Experience reveals, however, that the project is almost guaranteed to change in ways that neither partner fully anticipated. One way to address this is to build decision diamonds and checkpoints into the rollout of the outsourcing plan, and also to agree in advance on how to address changes as they occur.

Example: Flat Fee in Action

When TDS suddenly came into Compaq's life as the new outsourcing supplier, they negotiated a flat monthly fee. TDS tracked actual versus projected services. Even though they could have added on some additional charges, they chose not to. One of their immediate goals was to take the burden of detail off their partner, and one manifestation was their decision not to nickel-and-dime Compaq. Instead, they would take a look at the whole picture at renewal time. In fact, this model—and a similar philosophical approach—have been used in a number of outsourcing arrangements.

Fee Plus

In this variation on a flat-fee agreement, the company provides a fixed fee for an agreed-upon group of services, but then adds on incremental fees tied to volume or performance criteria, or both.

The advantage of such an agreement is that it protects both the supplier and the partner in good times and in bad. For the customer, there is a lower fixed portion, and therefore the opportunity to control costs, should the company experience a fiscal crisis. It also allows the customer to build in incentives for excellence and to modify the payments by volume as company populations and needs fluctuate. For the supplier, there is again the advantage of having certainty about a portion of its revenue. In addition, a conscientious supplier is likely to value the opportunity to build on that base through additional service volume or to enjoy some reward from meeting high performance standards.

On the downside, such an agreement can make financial planning more difficult for both partners. The financial structure may foster, among other things, a mentality of sudden spurts and stops, rather than a carefully planned and implemented strategy. As with the fixed-fee agreement, such problems can be anticipated and addressed through sound management of the partnership and the projects.

Usage Based

This is probably the most terrifying agreement for both customer and supplier, but it can work. In this arrangement, fees are tied directly to services delivered. There is no base. Typically, the trade-off for the vendor is that there is also no competition. In essence, they have guaranteed access to a ready market.

The primary advantage of this arrangement is that it provides enormous incentive for the supplier to market its services successfully within the company. This can be a real benefit to a company that is, for example, seeking to drive rapid deployment of a particular training initiative. With a hungry partner that is skilled in marketing as well as service delivery, this arrangement can be a real winner. The advantage to the supplier is obvious: a greater volume of business translates to larger profits.

The reason this approach strikes fear into the hearts of many customers and suppliers is its potential to spin wildly out of control. What if the vendor is "too successful" and breeds a large number of training-hungry employees within the company? What happens to the company's budget then? Alternatively, what if the individual customers are totally turned off by something a predecessor did, and no amount of skilled marketing will persuade them to buy? What if there are other roadblocks that make it impossible for the supplier to sell the services in which it has already invested substantial sums?

Again, although the potential for pain is very real in this model, the situation can be managed to make it successful for all. The same kind of candid discussion of expectations, agreement to an implementation plan and schedule, and checkpoints for what is going well, what is not, and what comes next—all surrounded by an atmosphere of complete candor and trust—can make it entirely possible for both partners to be entirely satisfied with a usage-based financial model.

Project Bid

This fee structure can be used alone or in combination with one of the fixed-fee models. In it, suppliers provide bids for defined services. Often these are competitive situations. In many cases, the other primary bidder is the customer itself—an internal training department.

Learning: Bids in Practice

Some partnerships have worked out a general framework that makes it possible for them to work together comfortably in an open-bid situation. In general, the partners agree that the supplier will handle the project if it has the expertise to do so and can provide it at lower cost than the customer's

---

> *internal department. While the supplier is not guaranteed the projects, they do have the opportunity to bid. The customer, on the other hand, provides feedback and information that enables the supplier to meet their expectations and standards. They all have some comfort in knowing that they have a long-term partnership, and at the same time accept the challenges of cost and quality competition.*

One advantage to this model is that it tends to hold costs down. It can also foster a competitive quest for excellence among the bidders. In addition, it often forces the customer to be extremely clear about needs and requirements, a factor that contributes heavily to the success of projects.

The disadvantages are that the bid process can generate a fair amount of work for the company. Notifying suppliers and reviewing proposals accounts for only part of the time and energy involved. A larger implication is that a company can wind up managing several different partners or, even more time consuming, a changing cast of partners with such an arrangement. It also has the potential to damage or destroy loyalty and responsiveness in partners. On the vendor's side, the bid process may create the kind of financial and staffing uncertainty that makes it extremely difficult to operate the organization.

Again, the problems can be managed by addressing them head-on, establishing ground rules by which the company and its pool of bidders operates. Limiting the number of bidders and providing ample information about future plans and opportunities can help both the company and the supplier to operate effectively with such a system.

There are some open questions affiliated with this approach. One is the question of audits. Should financial records be made available to the customer? Should guidelines on profitability be established? For a company with multiple training departments, should these units be required to participate in project monopolies? Based on experience, training organizations recommend against giving any single partner exclusive rights to bid on and render projects. On the other hand, partners always should have the opportunity to bid on projects for which they are qualified.

Develop a Training Strategy

Another area that deserves special attention in an outsourcing partnership is the training strategy. There are essentially two tiers of strategy. The first, described in chapter 2, is the initial strategy for outsourcing. This describes, among other things, the roles and responsibilities of each partner. For example, the company may decide to retain culture-related courses but hand off the skills-based courses to the partner. Or the company will retain content and course development but assign the delivery and logistics to its supplier.

Once this broad strategy is established and the partnership is launched, a second tier of strategies is needed. These must be developed for every project area, addressing the fundamental questions that affect each area's success. For example, both partners need to understand the direction in which the training function is headed. Will testing be added or improved? Will certification become an important tool in performance improvement or compensation? Is there a drive to improve performance objectives? Will changing needs create a demand for alternatives to traditional forms of training?

Answering such strategic questions leads to a body of standard practices. For example, they play out in training organizations in the nuts and bolts of establishing and applying training design standards, such as course objectives, testing for understanding, opportunities for practice, and structured feedback.

Handle Internal Staff Well

The odds for the success of an outsourcing venture appear to be visibly increased if the company's internal staff members are treated well. Even with the very best intentions, excellent skills, and sound planning, this is a sensitive and difficult area. Since outsourcing automatically implies (although does not always result in) some significant change in jobs, sometimes including the elimination of positions, staff members often greet outsourcing with fear, skepticism, and even downright hostility. Much of this can be ameliorated by direct, clear, and quick communication about the project and about its impact on employees.

Example: Worst Case

Any major change is accompanied by some horror stories, and the transition to outsourcing is certainly no exception. In many organizations, partnership managers on both sides lose sleep and dental enamel over one or a few disgruntled employees. If these people are left out of the early

---

> *communication loop, not treated with concern and consideration during the transition, or for other reasons of their own are unhappy about the new partnership, they can become powerful subversives. Often they have long-standing relationships with internal customers, and by dropping a "cautionary word" to these friends, can wittingly or unwittingly sabotage the outsourcing endeavor.*

Typically, there are several options for existing staff. These include the following: remaining in an internal training position but with a new responsibility, remaining with the company but transferring to another department, transferring to the staff of the outsourcing partner, providing similar services as an external contractor or consultant, or finally, leaving the company altogether. As suggested in chapter 2, creating a sound people strategy is a critical part of the transition. Experience reveals that the sooner rational, thoughtful people decisions can be made, the better for everyone.

When outsourcing partners speak candidly about their experiences, most admit that no matter how carefully and compassionately they have planned and managed the people changes, there is always opportunity for improvement. At Corning, where almost all of the staff wound up staying with the company, everyone wished that the new assignments had been provided faster. In other cases, where people were being asked to transfer to other positions in the company or move out of the company in one way or another, all agreed that it would have been impossible to make the moves too quickly, or with too much attention to the care of the people. On the other hand, Dow moved very quickly to transfer its employees to Delta, but their downfall was in not paying enough attention to qualifications or adequate preparation for the move, and it cost them dearly.

There are many steps that both partners can take to ease the transition. CCFL, for example, no longer has a population of salaried trainers. Rather, they contract with independent trainers, providing help to their customers' displaced employees in becoming consultants. They provide a major contract for two years to help these people get started as independent service providers. Having trainers who are knowledgeable about the company culture and programs provides a smooth and quick start-up. And the people who stay typically enjoy their jobs and are happy for the chance essentially to retain them, even with a change in their employment structure.

Communicate Forcefully with Suppliers

Just as it is to everyone's benefit to provide employees with prompt, honest information, it is also to everyone's benefit to communicate openly but forcefully with suppliers. At the earliest possible moment, the company should explain to its suppliers what the new arrangements are and how they will be expected to interface with the company and its chosen partner(s) under these arrangements. Certainly this is particularly critical when one supplier is assigned the role of managing other vendors on behalf of the company. Suppliers need to hear early and directly from their customers about the implications of such a transition to their business and relationship. If they are to be retained, the new relationship needs to be built. If they are not, they deserve the courtesy of knowing early, so that they can replace lost business or otherwise adjust to the change.

Like all major changes involving people, this one can be difficult. The benefits to prompt, honest communication are significant, however, and well worth the company's investment of forethought and planning. First, the outsourcing partners frequently want and need to maintain uninterrupted service to their customers, and this goal is more easily achieved by retaining those vendors who have a history of providing valued services. Experience in working together is hard to replace. Sometimes even finding another vendor with a comparable skills set at a comparable price is difficult. Second, the same kind of disruption that occurs with unhappy employees can occur with unhappy vendors. Suppliers who feel threatened have been known to react with fear, jealousy, anger, and a whole range of other negative emotions. As a result, they can damage the new outsourcing venture. They may try to appeal the decision, which can be time consuming and messy. Or they can extend their hurt into their relationships with the training department's internal customers, damaging the outsourcing supplier before the project even gets off the ground. Internal resistance generated in this way certainly can slow down the transition and deflect energy from where it is needed in start-up. Therefore, open communication among vendors is critical. It should include introductory letters, individual phone calls, and at least one group meeting as well as periodic assessments. In spite of such attempts at communication, some vendors will insist on contacting the company directly, often giving a presentation about their services that includes broad hints that they would be a better outsourcing partner. In some cases, nothing will make these vendors content.

Build and Maintain Trust

Trust is essential for most outsourcing relationships. It may be slightly less an issue for partnerships that center on specific, limited services that can be quantified: a call center for registration, for example. But even then, a strong relationship between the partners is important, not only for its own sake but because so many other functions depend on it. Because new relationships are fraught with so many disparate factors and uncertainties, however, building trust among all the parties can be difficult. Leaving even a single person outside the corral can be surprisingly harmful to the whole effort.

Some elements of building a trust strategy are detailed in chapter 2. Other literature and a number of consultants deal almost exclusively and in depth with this critical and difficult area. One of the issues is that *feeling* trust does not automatically translate to *conveying* it. Thus the whole matter of open, honest, and frequent communication is intimately linked to trust, as is a whole range of other behaviors: shared planning, accountability, and recognition, for example.

Every successful partnership is built on trust. Some that have failed would cite this as one reason. In these cases, the issue is not necessarily one of dishonesty or ill-intent, but rather the behaviors that enable partners to rely on one another. Thus, developing a strategy for building trust and testing all other parts of the plan and relationship against the factors that help to build or destroy it will be worth the investment of time and resources.

So far, this chapter has touched on seven factors that have been shown to strongly influence success and five more that deserve special attention because they have often proved difficult to do well. Now it is time to turn to those that can doom a project.

THE KISS OF DEATH

Some of the factors that fall into this category may be surprising. At first glance, they may seem like annoyances or minor management mistakes, but experience reveals that in fact they can be fatal. Projects with the following symptoms will always fail, unless the partners intervene quickly and decisively:

- Exclusive focus on details.
- Testing the relationship.

- Pervasive fear in the training department.
- No baseline data or documented processes.

Exclusive Focus on Details

In one situation, a supplier's representatives sat through endless partnership meetings that focused exclusively and exhaustively on the number of courses, dates, starting and stopping times, and other details. After they thought they were set to roll, they uncovered an issue that stopped them cold. It turned out that the company mistrusted the entire development function. Not only had the supplier and the company representatives never discussed this, there was never an inkling of a problem. This single experience, although extraordinarily distressing, provided a never-to-be-forgotten learning experience. Many outsourcing partners have similar tales to tell. Kaiser Permanente's first outsourcing relationship fell victim to several fatal flaws, but this was certainly among them. There are elements of this in one of Compaq's early partnership endeavors, too.

Learning: A Technique for Tracking Progress

Because it is so easy to hone in on detail, and because this requires the opposite kind of thinking to strategic thinking, partners should hold separate but parallel meetings on strategy and logistics. This simple separation enables partners to focus effectively on both.

Such difficulties are more likely to be prevented if the entire partnership team develops and maintains an overall view. By establishing checkpoints that are not simply clerical, but aligned with the larger goals and strategy, team members provide a structure for measuring progress. Virtually every aspect of the relationship should appear on this list: the content of the courses, the learning outcomes, the instruction, the progress toward major goals, the evaluation and measurement processes and learnings, and much more. Such a strategy and plan helps partners to ensure that they not only stay on top of the minutiae but also ask the big questions regularly. In this process, suppliers will do well to actively seek understanding of what their partners are happy with, what they are unhappy with, and what is nagging at the back of their minds that might surface as a future issue.

Testing the Relationship

Sometimes it pays to devote attention to subtle, intuitive factors. Problems that develop between partners do not always surface in an open, honest manner. For whatever reason, an important player in a partnership occasionally appears to hope for its failure. Sometimes the manifestations of this are obvious: Anger erupts, blame is assigned, phone messages are repeatedly ignored. At other times, the symptoms are more subtle: Information is withheld, jokes have just a little barb, rumors begin to surface. In either case, there is trouble afoot.

Lack of commitment to the project manifested in such "testing" behavior is almost always the hardest to address. If only the person would be candid and express a willingness to deal with the problem, others could tackle it. But veiled malice—whether consciously or subconsciously intended—is a dangerous poison, and antidotes are uncertain. The particular means of addressing the issue will be dictated by the particular scenario and players. The one certainty is that, left unaddressed, this poison will be lethal. Swift, direct action is essential. At times, even this cannot save the partnership. But usually it is worth the risk, because inattention will almost certainly allow the disease to run to an inevitable conclusion.

Pervasive Fear in the Training Department

A related problem is pervasive fear in the training department. This too can undermine an outsourcing project in short order. One of the usual manifestations of this fear as it advances is that information is withheld, crippling the ability to address issues, take corrective action, or even celebrate legitimate successes.

A sound and thorough people strategy can do much to check fears early on, and then to prevent them from resurfacing as the partnership develops. Again, key elements of the plan are clear, honest, and frequent communication. Particularly important are communication of the rationale for outsourcing and the decisions that have been made. Staff members need to know why the decision to outsource meets the company's business objectives, as well as which issues are open for discussion and debate and which are not. Having skilled managers of people and meetings in place can go a long way toward allaying fears and moving the project and the people forward. Leaders who kindly but firmly insist on moving along the charted course, while also letting employees know that they are heard, understood, and valued, are worth every cent they are paid.

No Baseline Data or Documented Processes

Here is another issue that, like the exclusive focus on detail, may appear to be a smaller problem than it really is. Baseline data on virtually every outsourcing objective is essential. The rationale for this is clear: If a company does not fully understand how well it is doing, it has no basis for judging a service provider. The absence of baseline data leads to a whole range of ills: broken and unrepaired systems, muffed explanations, misread results, hand-offs that go awry, and more.

Similarly, a clear document describing every process is equally important. In order to transfer its operations successfully, the company must understand precisely how each of its important tasks (and many of its minor ones) is accomplished. This means not only having process maps or written procedures but also knowing that these accurately reflect what really happens on a daily basis. The absence of correct documentation has been the cause of innumerable errors, lost time, and failed relationships.

The example cited below reflects one of the problems that can occur. There are many, many more. Fortunately, this is a preventable problem. The downside, however, is that it is usually not possible to remedy it after the fact. Then the decision becomes how to start over and begin with fresh data or new processes. But such new starts suffer from old wounds.

Example: More Data, More Data!

Kaiser Permanente's first partnership ended before it got off the ground. There were multiple reasons, not the least of which was that they were attempting something that had not been done by an organization of its mammoth size and very unique needs. One of the issues that surfaced early in those discussions, however, was a disagreement between the partners about baseline data. KP had done rather extensive internal research on the types, quantities, and delivery systems for their multiple, decentralized training activities. They realized that their information was not complete, but they believed their information was comprehensive enough for them to proceed. Their partner, however, wanted to conduct additional

---

assessments. They believed that they could not provide what was needed unless they had a clearer picture of what existed. They also were concerned about being held accountable against a standard that was unclear. And there were financial implications all around. Probably KP did not have enough data. Probably the provider was utilizing too much time and money in gathering more than was actually needed. In any case, this became one of several serious issues that ultimately caused this partnership to collapse.

In the context of the repeated theme of the prevention of potential problems comes a strong recommendation for partners to delay the actual start-up of the partnership until the data is collected and tested for accuracy. This will require strong will power. It is tedious and painful to go back and analyze systems or piece together results when all parties are energized toward moving ahead. Stopping to get data feels a lot like putting on the brakes, and in fact, it can be burdensome and psychologically difficult to manage. But it is well worth this delay to prevent the future ones that are all too likely to be even more serious and damaging to the project.

The "kiss of death" may sound melodramatic, but in fact the young history of outsourcing has been fraught with fatal errors. This section has endeavored to translate those into fatal error messages. With these warnings, prospective partners may be able to better anticipate what might appear on their screens, what to do if such messages do occur, and better still, what measures might help to preclude them ever seeing these dire words.

THE FINAL WORD: SYSTEM

This review of outsourcing in training, education, and development comes back to the same word again and again: system. An outsourcing partnership comes to life and remains healthy only because it is constructed as a unique organism that meets the particular needs and capitalizes on the particular strengths of all partners. A new entity is created, with a new organization, structure, and mission. Its success depends, more than anything else, on the development, regular review, and deployment of systems that are linked to strategies, and that clearly and precisely align the operational details that allow the effort to function effectively.

Developing the right system begins with many questions. For the company, the questions focus largely on their own needs and how a vendor might meet them and fit with their organization. What will work for our organization? What can effectively be outsourced or out-tasked? How do we want to work with our partner(s)? Will we think of them as vendors, colleagues, or partners? What will be the style of our relationship? Will it be formal, informal, or downright casual? Will we meet around a conference table or go out for a beer, or some of both? Where are we headed with our training and development function? How will it make the most meaningful contributions to our company's goals? What are our partners' responsibilities within the training and development function? How do we build a sense of pride and ownership in our partner? How should our partner interact with internal customers? What are our partners' rights with relation to our project work? How will we anticipate changes and handle unexpected developments? How will we deal with breakdowns and problems? How will we maintain a healthy environment for education and development as this change takes place? How can we build our own learning into this relationship?

Ultimately these questions and others feed into the following three decision systems:

- Decisions about process: How will we go about outsourcing?
- Decisions about outcome: What do we want our new structure to produce?
- Decisions about relationship: How do we want to work with our providers?

For the service provider, the questions are slightly different, but asking them and answering them well is equally as important as that process is for the customer. Sometimes the very best decision is to walk away from opportunities that are not right for the provider, and the only way to do that is to seek answers to a lot of questions.

For suppliers, the questions fall into similar categories as the company's, but with a different slant. The vendor needs to understand the company's needs and culture in order to assess the fit with its own capabilities and style. What is the company presently doing in its training, education, and development endeavor? Why are they seeking to outsource? Are their goals for outsourcing clear and realistic? What is their vision for the future? How clearly and fully have they considered their own function in relation to their management's strategic direction? What changes in direction are foreseeable that will affect training and development? What problems have they had, and how have they addressed them? What is their organizational style and culture? Are the behavior patterns consistent from one part of the company to another or are there major differences among different employee groups? Where is the company located? What part(s) of their operations are they seeking to outsource? Are they looking to use one or several partners? If there are to be several, how do they envision them interfacing? What kind of management do they intend to provide? What are their expectations? How open do they seem in providing information and discussing approaches and ideas they may not have considered? Who would be the key players? What do we bring to the party?

Again, these and more questions enable a supplier to do the essential analysis in the following areas:

- Decisions on fit: How do our capabilities, strengths, values, and style fit with their needs and culture?

- Decisions on outcome: What would be the form of our working together?

- Decisions about relationships: How will we work with our customer and other vendors, if there are several partners?

As these decisions are made and systems to support them developed, a new entity will begin to emerge. And as this happens, the partners will experience the excitement, frustrations, and surprises that accompany such a metamorphosis. At some point, it will be necessary for both partners to step back from their roles as separate organizations and recognize the outsourcing partnership as a new creature. This is another of those outsourcing "moments"— an intuitive discovery of the reality of the new entity. Such a moment is impossible to quantify. It is critical, however. A review of the successful outsourcing ventures affirms that real success in this realm occurs only when these partnerships do take on a life of their own, with defined processes, outcomes, relationships, and all of the other elements of an organic system.

CONCLUSION

Newcomers to the prospect of outsourcing who are reading these lists of questions may feel overwhelmed. They would not be unjustified. These are complex decisions and relationships, and a great deal rides on their success—for all of the prospective partners.

When outsourcing partnerships work well, the results can be enormously rewarding for everyone concerned. Companies can enjoy a level and variety of training and development expertise that few can afford to hire and maintain. They can see results in employee learning that exceed their expectations. They can and do save money—actually in rather substantial amounts, although again, this should not be the primary goal or focus. And by divesting themselves of some tasks, they are better able to focus on their mission.

There are rewards for providers, too. Training providers are, at heart, oriented to service, and particularly to learning. Being able to provide excellent service and to know that learning has resulted is what makes some of them spring out of bed in the morning and go home contented at night. For many of them, the rewards are far more a matter of personal satisfaction than money. Nevertheless, there are now a number of firms in the outsourcing arena that also measure their success in terms of profitability, and by those measures, too, they are finding rewards in this business.

As for the future, it would seem that strategic direction and "reliance on special expertise" will prevail as themes after the year 2000. Whatever lies ahead, it is hoped that the experiences and learnings shared in this book will help others to make sound decisions about whether to outsource, or to improve their existing outsourcing partnerships. Like all good partnerships, may this book offer significant expertise, provide context, and inspire dreams.

APPENDICES

APPENDIX 1. ENSURING PERFORMANCE STANDARDS

CONTRACT TEMPLATE

CCFL Instructor Agreement

(When we contract with an independent consultant/trainer who has his/her own program already developed, that is "buying off the shelf.")

(1) This agreement is between _____, henceforth "instructor," and College Center of the Finger Lakes, henceforth "CCFL."

(2) Instructor desires to instruct and CCFL desires to provide instructor's services to the employees of Corning Incorporated. [other employers/CCFL's customers, including . . .]

(3) Instructor will present in [Corning, New York], a course named _____ on _____ to start at _____ and end at _____. This contract will apply to subsequent programs presented by instructor for CCFL. [may be modified]

(4) Instructor will provide one set of course notes, with clear objectives and camera ready, to CCFL at least [three] weeks prior to the above date for CCFL's reproduction for each participant. CCFL reserves the right to assure quality. Instructor warrants that none of the material used will violate the copyright of others. CCFL is granted by instructor onetime reproduction permission of submitted materials, and CCFL agrees that materials will not be used for any other commercial purposes beyond the education of the students present in the class.

(5) CCFL will pay the instructor $_____ (per day/per program). Additionally, travel and living expenses will be reimbursable upon presentation of an invoice with receipts. CCFL will pay under this contract within thirty (30) days of receipt of final billing. (See attached expense guidelines.) Instructor is responsible for making all travel and hotel reservations.

(6) Nothing in this document is to be construed as an employer-employee relationship. Instructor will be serving as an independent contractor, and, as such, will alone be responsible for withholding, taxes, FICA, etc.

(7) CCFL will market, advertise, and recruit participants for the workshop. However, if it is determined that there is insufficient enrollment, CCFL reserves the right to cancel this course without penalty up to four weeks prior to the first day of the course. CCFL will work with the instructor when making this decision.

(8) Instructor agrees that all requests from clients for service (including but not limited to seminars, in-house seminars and training programs, consulting, conference facilitation) must be routed to CCFL. In no case will the instructor be compensated directly by a client for services rendered under the auspices of CCFL. Failure to convey client service request or circumvention of the fee/billing process will be considered a violation of the working agreement between an instructor and CCFL and will result in immediate termination of the agreement.

(9) Instructor agrees not to overtly and explicitly sell a product or service with which he/she is associated or from which he/she can financially benefit.

(10) Instructor agrees not to divulge information identified as proprietary to any other person or corporation.

(11) Instructor agrees not to offer similar programs on an open enrollment basis within [eighteen months] of CCFL's program with a [150 mile] radius of Corning, New York.

(12) Instructor agrees to support and demonstrate commitment to valuing diversity. [See attached memo on diversity.]

Please indicate your acceptance of this agreement by returning one signed copy to us in the envelope provided within 15 days. Receipt of this signed agreement is necessary for instructor to receive payment as indicated in paragraph 5 above.

Garry J. DeRose, Director
College Center of the Finger Lakes

Date:

Agreed and Accepted by: _____
                          (name, title)

                        _____
                           (company)

                        _____
                            (date)

PROCESS CHANGE DOCUMENT

Course _____

Date _____ Originator _____

Change from:

Change to:

Does this change affect other parts of this course or other courses? If so, what?

Reason for change:

Approvals: Signature and dates

Quality Education Mgr._____ Quality Director_____

CCFL Director _____ CCFL Coordinator_____

Document Number _____ PCD Number _____

_____
Copyright © College Center of the Finger Lakes

ASSURING THE QUALITY AND FIT OF GENERIC TRAINING WORKSHOPS

When purchasing previously developed workshops from suppliers, extra care must be taken to assure that the specific needs of your audience are met. Unlike workshops that are developed in-house and frequently repeated for your company, packaged workshops typically do not enjoy the benefits of audience-familiar instructors, local support, and continuous feedback-modification loops. To compensate, workshop coordinators should:

1. Define requirements pertaining to topic, learner(s), price, duration, and sponsor:
   - ☐ Use E&T Search service to identify 3 to 5 alternative solutions.
   - ☐ Identify contacts within population to be trained. Get preliminary input from them and let them know that you may request their help again, as delivery time approaches.

2. Focus on tangibles:
   - ☐ Use form letter to request written proposals addressing objectives, learning activities, sample agenda, intended audience, presenter credentials, and planned follow-up. Proposals should be results-oriented and specific.
   - ☐ Demand to see workshop materials, including transparencies, in advance.

3. Get references:
   - ☐ Ask supplier to provide list of references, including contact person, address, and telephone number.
   - ☐ Ask each reference to name others who have used the same workshop. Contact them too.
   - ☐ Contact three references per supplier. Ask direct questions about details, satisfaction, shortcomings, and whether they would rehire. Ask if presenters understood and related to audience.
   - ☐ Try to attend same workshop at another site, or ask to see a videotape of the presenter in action.

4. Select the best alternative and complete the paperwork:
   - ☐ Send the "consultant's package," including the standard contract.
   - ☐ Review your specific situation and then send specific written elaborations of any requirements not sufficiently covered in the contract. These may include requirements for content, delivery, professionalism, or "money back if not satisfied" guarantees.

5. Check in with your contacts:
   - ☐ Have your contacts review materials, giving feedback and suggestions. Arrange for pre-course telephone conversation between in-company contacts and presenter.

6. Help the instructor and the workshop to fit in:
   - ☐ Two weeks before workshop, review agenda in detail with instructor. Ensure appropriate delivery for expected audience. (Remind instructor that all points must be covered but flexibility should be maintained with regard to depth.)
   - ☐ Send instructor participant roster and info on company(ies), including major businesses, organizational structure, and values.
   - ☐ Review requirements for room setup, equipment, etc.
   - ☐ Have established local person introduce presenter.
   - ☐ Require workshop to start with distribution of agenda and objectives. Next, gather participants' expectations.
   - ☐ Require instructor to do brief "process check" after first quarter of workshop, gathering feedback on coverage, pace, etc.
   - ☐ Have instructor use examples that demonstrate familiarity with audience and company.
   - ☐ Revisit objectives and expectations before distributing participant reaction forms at conclusion.
   - ☐ Even if instructor is an experienced expert, form your own independent judgments as to what is required and ensure that these requirements are met.

PROGRAM/MODULE CHECKLIST

Does the program/module include . . ?

1. Performance Objectives
   - Are they measurable? _____
   - Are they explained clearly prior to the instruction? _____
   - Are learners made aware that competent performance of the objective (skill) directly affects the company and themselves in a positive manner? _____

2. Practice
   - Does the practice activity match or approximate the objective (skill) as it would be performed in the work environment (that is, are the conditions the same; are they using the same tools, machines, materials, and process they will on the job)? _____
   - Is feedback on the practice performance provided (reinforcing desired actions and behaviors or suggesting corrections for undesirable actions and behaviors)? _____

3. Examples and Nonexamples
   - Do the learners know what competent performance of the objective (skill) looks like? _____
   - Do the learners know what incompetent performance of the objective (skill) looks like? _____

4. Skill Checks (criterion-referenced test items)
   - Are skill-check tests provided to measure learning? _____
   - Does performance of the skill-check test match the performance of the objective (skill)? _____
   - Does skill-check performance match or approximate the objective (skill) as it would be performed in the work environment? _____

5. Content
   - Does the content represent the gap between what the learners already know and what they need to know to perform the objective (skill)? _____

6. Support Items
   - Have you selected support items (work materials, equipment, overheads, workbooks, etc.) that provide the features called for by your objectives? _____

7. Transition to the Workplace
   - Are there procedures, processes, or job aids in the module that enable the employee to, and ensure they are, using the objective (skill) on the job in the future? _____

8. Restatement of the Objectives
   - Prior to conclusion of the module, are the objectives reviewed? _____
   - If so, is it communicated to the learner how each was met? _____

TIPS FOR SUCCESS

These tips are the result of a compilation of previous end-of-course reactions. Please read and use them.

Before Class:

☐ Send a one-page biography to CCFL for inclusion in materials or special requests.

☐ Send clear, actionable course objectives to CCFL.

☐ Study Corning Incorporated diversity materials; be prepared to avoid stereotypes, gender, or racial comments.

During Class:

☐ Ask for the participants' expectations up front.

☐ Provide and represent clear, actionable objectives.

☐ Discuss the agenda and follow it as closely as possible.

☐ Demonstrate your knowledge of Corning Incorporated (quality commitment, history, values) early and often.

☐ Be vigilant about diversity issues. Avoid stereotypes, gender, or racial comments. Discourage the participants from using them.

☐ Begin the session punctually and end it on time.

☐ Do process checks throughout the day. Ask if the participants are comfortable (hot, cold, and so forth); ask if the pace is good; ask if the material is understandable.

☐ Use many up-to-date, relevant examples (Corning-specific where appropriate). Also include examples applicable to the participants' jobs.

☐ Be energetic and excited about your topic while maintaining a sincere approach.

☐ Encourage participant involvement by asking questions.

☐ Use break-out rooms if possible or applicable to your material.

☐ Use break times to connect with the participants (mingle, get to know their names).

☐ Give scheduled breaks, and if the participants appear to need an unscheduled break, it is better to give them one than to lose their attention.

☐ Class time may not be used to sell products or services with which you are associated or from which you can financially benefit.

At the End of Class:

☐ Close the workshop with an overview. Ask the participants if they are satisfied and if their expectations have been met.

☐ Ask the participants to write down or share how they believe they will be able to use on the job what they have just learned.

☐ Give the participants time to complete the reaction form and encourage them to do so.

APPENDIX 2: OUTSOURCING THE TRAINING FUNCTION CHECKLIST

Commit to "Re" Sourcing

☐ Have you identified your hopes and fears?

☐ Draft your project plan.

☐ Do you have a clear mission statement for the training and education operation?

☐ Have you identified a strategic direction?

☐ Have you identified your current, major processes?
— Can you identify the processes necessary to carry out the strategic mission?
— Have you benchmarked these processes?
— Can you tell which of those processes must be done internally?
— In which do you have expertise that exceeds those of other organizations?
— Which do you believe that you could outsource?

☐ What is your purpose for outsourcing?
— Reduce costs
— Sharpen strategic focus
— Add expertise
— Provide comprehensive services

☐ Write these purposes as objectives:

_____

_____

_____

_____

☐ What would you consider success? How would you measure it?

_____

_____

_____

_____

Select Activities to Outsource

☐ What are your basic tasks?

☐ What are your sources?

☐ What are the pros and cons of your sources?

☐ What activities will you select for outsourcing?

☐ What improvement will you make?

☐ What are your baseline measures?

Decide on Supplier(s)

☐ What are your supplier selection criteria?

☐ Who are your potential providers?

☐ Have you rated the overall capabilities and capacity of the suppliers? Will they be able to do 100 percent of the outsourced tasks?

☐ Rate and comment on the outsource's systems and processes:
  — Value system
  — Financial system
  — Recruiting system
  — Process documentation
  — Marketing

☐ Rate and comment on the outsource's:
  — Stability
  — Experience
  — Reputation

☐ How long has the outsourcer been performing the function?

☐ How do the provider's costs compare to internal costs?

☐ How much current business is already with the provider?

☐ How fast can they achieve a full service level for you?

- ☐ Does the supplier use the latest technology?
- ☐ Are the provider's systems documented?
- ☐ Does the provider have a solid training system for its own employees?
- ☐ Does the provider have a solid recruiting system and record?
- ☐ What systems does the supplier have in place to work with its suppliers?
- ☐ What is your decision?

Contract for Services

- ☐ What are your goals and performance measures?
- ☐ What are your requirements?
- ☐ What is your change process?
- ☐ Does the contract:
    - — Describe the services to be provided?
    - — Establish standards of performance?
    - — Establish remedies if standards are not met?
    - — Describe the back-up system in case of disaster?
    - — Require that proprietary material be handled properly?
- ☐ Does the contract cover:
    - — Systems for handling changes in requirements?
    - — Pricing?
    - — Terms of engagement?
    - — Deconverting?
    - — Limitations on liability?
    - — Scheduling start-up?
    - — Intellectual property rights?
    - — Personnel—can staff be hired from each other?
    - — Termination?

Transition Activities

- ☐ Do you have a transition project plan with decision diamonds?
- ☐ Have you completed a potential problem analysis on it?
- ☐ Do you have a customer strategy?
- ☐ Is your people strategy in place?

- [ ] Is your transition structured to build trust and positive relationships among team members?
- [ ] Is an internal/outsource project team in place and functioning?
- [ ] Is it structured to build trust and positive relationships among team members?
- [ ] Is there joint decision making?
- [ ] Do internal and outsource staff include one another in staff meetings?
- [ ] Are the transition states planned?
- [ ] How is the outsource team being educated?
- [ ] Is there a new area for internal staff to focus on?
- [ ] Has agreement been reached on how to make the transfer "transparent" to the customers?
- [ ] How is world-class quality performance assured?
- [ ] What is the plan for evaluation?

Manage

- [ ] Who is your partnership manager?

Monitor and Improve

- [ ] What tools do you have in place for continuous improvement?
- [ ] What are your monitoring and improvement processes?

APPENDIX 3: CUSTOMER SATISFACTION SCORECARD

A1: Registration and Materials

1. Did you reach CCFL immediately when you contacted them? If not, please explain.
2. Did you receive a confirmation e-mail reminder before your class?
3. On a scale of 1–7, what would you rate the calendar and other training materials provided, in terms of helpfulness and the information provided? Any comments?
4. Do you have any thoughts or comments about your experience with CCFL, positive or negative?
5. On a scale of 1–7, rate your overall satisfaction with registering for training.
6. Could you think of any areas where your team could use customized training?

A2: Interview re: E&T Search

1. Were you pleased with the choices CCFL gave you on the topic for which you were searching?
2. Did CCFL find you this class in a timely manner?
3. Was the cost of the class an influence on your choice?
4. Did the class end up being what you expected or what you had in mind?
5. On a scale of 1–7, please rate your overall satisfaction with CCFL's customer service during the E&T Search.
6. Please tell us about any of your thoughts or comments, either positive or negative, about using the E&T Search.
7. On a scale of 1–7, please rate your overall satisfaction with the E&T Search system.

A3: Interview re: Customized Classes

1. Why did you request a customized class?
2. Did CCFL find you this class in a timely manner?
3. On a scale of 1–7, please rate how satisfied you were with the process of finding this class through CCFL.
4. On a scale of 1–7, please rate how satisfied you were with the actual class. Did the class suit your needs as you expected?
5. Please tell us any of your thoughts or comments, either positive or negative, about using the E&T Search.

ABOUT THE AUTHOR

As the director of CCFL since 1981, Garry J. DeRose has guided its dramatic growth in size and approach. From its early stage as a supplier of training and education courses to a restricted local audience, CCFL has evolved to its current position as a national supplier of broad-based training, education, and development services. In 1987 he began working closely with CCFL's largest long-term customer to create a partnership that has become a model for outsourcing alliances nationwide. The new organization, CCFL/Corning, became Corning's supplier for both administration and delivery of employee training. Since beginning the partnership with Corning, CCFL has become the outsourcing partner for other companies as well.

In addition to guiding the development of these relationships and overseeing their ongoing success, Garry has also assisted a number of *Fortune* 500 companies in designing and implementing outsourcing arrangements with other suppliers. He has also helped many businesses and training organizations move from traditional customer-vendor relationships centered narrowly on training events to broader-based partnerships focused on learning and development.

As a respected expert on the subject of outsourcing, he has written articles and presented numerous lectures and discussions based on his own experience, participated in extensive discussions with leaders of national projects, and published literature on the topic. Popular with his audiences for his humor and insights during discussion as well as for his in-depth understanding of outsourcing, he is regularly invited to speak at conferences sponsored by such organizations as the American Society for Training & Development, the International Society for Performance Improvement, and the International Quality and Productivity Council.

Garry holds Ph.D. and M.A. degrees from the University of Wisconsin, a B.A. from Montclair (New Jersey) State College, and an M.B.A. in marketing from Syracuse University. He also holds certificates in Marketing Management, Managerial Decision Making, Project Management, Management of Life-Long Learning, and German Language Studies.